Arlene –
All the best!

Kaylee

Wiley Global Finance is a market-leading provider of over 400 annual books, mobile applications, elearning products, workflow training tools, newsletters and websites for both professionals and consumers in institutional finance, trading, corporate accounting, exam preparation, investing, and performance management.

www.wileyglobalfinance.com

WILEY Global Finance
WHERE DATA FINDS DIRECTION

WEALTH REGENERATION AT RETIREMENT

WEALTH REGENERATION AT RETIREMENT

Planning for a Lifetime of Leadership

Kaycee Krysty

with

Robert Moser

BLOOMBERG PRESS
An Imprint of
⊛WILEY

Library of Congress Cataloging-in-Publication Data:

Krysty, Kaycee W. author.
 Wealth regeneration at retirement : planning for a lifetime of leadership/Kaycee Krysty with
Robert Moser.
  pages cm. — (Bloomberg financial series)
  Includes index.
  ISBN 978-1-118-27656-3 (cloth); ISBN 978-1-118-33340-2 (ebk);
  ISBN 978-1-118-33129-3 (ebk); ISBN 978-1-118-33057-9 (ebk)
   1. Retirement—United States—Planning.   2. Retirement income—United States.
3. Executives—United States.   4. Baby boom generation—United States.   I. Moser, Robert,
author.   II. Title.
HQ1063.2.U6K79 2013
306.3'80973—dc23
                                                              2012020165

Printed in the United States of America

10 9 8 7 6 5 4 3 2 1

MIX
Paper from
responsible sources

FSC
www.fsc.org

FSC® C005928

For our spouses, Michael and Candy, the people in our lives who hold us accountable and keep us turning the wheel forward. Thanks for all the nudging!

Contents

Acknowledgments

This book would not have been possible without the help, support, and wisdom of many people.

First we would like to acknowledge the Laird Norton family. Their openness and rigor in stewarding both their human and financial capital are an inspiration every day. They set the standard for Wealth Regeneration®.

We would also like to acknowledge our many clients over the years who have taught us so much about what it means to lead a generative life and leave a positive legacy. They allowed us to push them and prod them, asking all the difficult questions that went into formulating the ideas presented in this book. We have been honored to be their partner as they plan for Wealth Regeneration. A particular thanks goes to those clients of long standing (and you know who you are) who were willing co-experimenters when we were just taking baby steps.

So many professional colleagues have helped along the way that it is impossible to mention them all. Our desire is to reciprocate, so that more and more individuals and families have good counsel on the road ahead. We would like to particularly acknowledge Jay Hughes, whose many years of mentorship and substantive writings have so clearly informed our work; Bill George, whose work on authenticity has inspired a generation of business leaders; and Pamela MacLean and Frederick Hudson, whose clear-eyed view of change sets the stage for facing the future with intention.

And finally our sincere appreciation to our colleagues at Laird Norton Tyee. Wealth Regeneration is a team sport, and we are privileged to play on the same team as some of the best in the business. To quote Theodore Roosevelt: "Far and away the best prize that life offers is the chance to work hard at work worth doing." At Laird Norton Tyee we get to do that every day.

Kaycee and Bob
June 2012

Foreword

Generativity or Stagnation? These are the two states of being, the great psychologist Erik H. Erikson, in his book *Childhood and Society*, offers to those of us either entering or living in the third stage of life. How stark and yet how accurate these two terms are for defining our lives from about 60 to 80. Don't worry that I am cutting your life short; there is another stage for 80–100, where the two options are Ego Integrity and Despair. Getting the Generative self right creates a high probability that you will have one more stage, the stage of Ego Integrity, toward leaving this life fulfilled and flourishing right to the final second. Despair as the state of one's being at the end of life? Unthinkable!!!

The book you are about to read offers a path to Generativity that is bold. Equally, it requires all of the dedication, passion, and creativity you brought to the first two stages of your life; the stage of youth and adolescence, the stage of learning; and the second stage of vocation and relationship, the stage of doing. It is a journey of transition that will ask you once again to shed your shell (in this case of your second stage) as you once shed the shell of your first-stage self, so you can create a new larger shell to accommodate your larger more deeply aware third-stage self.

In my opinion very little useful information has been offered so far to the 70 million of you, known as Baby Boomers (those born between 1/1/1946–12/31/1962), to help you understand the path to Generativity; the way of being that the third stage of life is all about. Equally, the fear of stagnation that the "R" (Retirement) word defines has gotten lots of worried press. Appreciating this reality, Kaycee Krysty and Bob Moser have offered a set of diagnostics and a path to apply them that, if followed with dedication and discernment, will lead you to be the Generative person this stage of life calls you to be.

I can well imagine that many of you have the same fear of loss of your dynamism that I felt when I reached 60, for me exactly 10 years ago. Perhaps unlike you, I was so worried about it that I decided to read all I could on the third stage of life. I can also tell you that I knew, as you do, that this stage of life was often defined as the Senior stage of life, or Codger stage, and this really frightened me. However, in watching my parents live through this stage, I saw them become true Elders and never Seniors. So in my reading I sought to discover what the third stage of "being" and "giving back" was about. I sought to determine why and how I could make conscious choices, using a seriously meaningful set of actions that would lead to my becoming a true Elder and never a Codger.

Where did the journey lead me? To Aristotle, in the *Nichomachean Ethics* and its journey to happiness; to many of the wisdom teachers in the various spiritual systems on our planet who I discovered were our Elders, our true wisdom keepers; to Dante and his *Divine Comedy* and within it Dante's gift that reminds us that there are times when we find ourselves in a dark wood with no way out, a dark wood from which we can only extract ourselves by our willingness to call our metaphorical Virgils to life to lead us to Generativity; to Sigmund Freud; to Carl Jung; to James Hillman's *The Soul's Code;* to James Hollis's *Finding Meaning in the Second Half of Life* and *The Middle Passage;* to Jane R. Pretat's *Coming of Age;* to John R. O'Neil's and Allan Jones's *Seasons of Grace;* to Daniel Levinson's *The Seasons of a Man's Life* and *The Seasons of a Woman's Life;* to Michael Meade's *Men and the Water of Life;* to Barbara G. Walker's *Crone;* to Gail Sheehey's *New Passages;* to Angeles Arrien; to Rabbi Shalomi-Schachter's *Ageing to Sageing;* and finally to those who spoke to me most profoundly—Erik H. Erickson and above all Abraham Maslow and his *Towards a Psychology of Being.*

Why was and is Maslow my greatest teacher? Because he defines the hierarchy of one's life's development and its highest achievement, its apogee, its fully grown third stage, as that of practicing altruism in all that one does. Essentially, it is: the stage of giving back to those we love and to our society—to become Good Samaritans; to be more productive than we have ever been before. I believe he is right about ultimate success in how to live one's life and the happiness that will be afforded to us it if we should succeed.

I decided, after I read Maslow, that his was the path of development I would adopt for this new stage of MY life—a path of development that I believed might, if I was diligent and discerning, lead me successfully to the "being" stage of life, to becoming a true Elder. I wanted to learn to grow myself toward his idea of being. Above all I wanted to ensure I was not falling into Stagnation and Despair; that I was becoming Generative.

I hasten to say that I tell my story only in the hope that it may encourage you to find your own way of understanding and expressing this stage of life and the lineage that underlies it. The important thing is to get going in finding YOUR way by learning from the wisdom keepers whose voices you discover you can hear best.

These last ten years I have been working on being Generative, seeking to understand and live the role of an Elder while doing all I can not to be a Codger. Toward this end and toward exploring the issues of this stage of life I have written extensively on wealth, family, and the role of Elders in family and in society, including the roles in family of active grandparents.[1]

In these works, I challenge you to consider your role in your own family at this stage of your life. As an Elder your actions can help deepen your family's sense of its own uniqueness. You can tell the family stories and remind the family of shared core values. As an Elder you're in a unique position to bring to your family the seventh-generation wisdom of the Iroquois that said "it should be our hope that the care and thoughtfulness we bring to our decision-making today will be remembered and honored by our descendents seven generations from today."

Further, I suggest that senior generations should ask, "What role can I have in the family that keeps me active and participating in a way that is appropriate to my seniority but does not cripple the growth and leadership of my children?"

I have outlined my journey for you as I hope it might offer you confidence that some who have gone before you on their journeys into this stage of life are successfully navigating it. It is also my way of welcoming you to this stage of life. I hope that as it supports you, you will play the wisdom forward as exemplified in your successful navigation of this stage of life's twists and turns, as you learn to live Generatively and become the true Elder you are destined to be.

I love this stage of life and so far the disaster of Stagnation that Erickson offers as the shadow side of it has never overtaken me. I am certain that if you follow Kaycee and Bob's journey and keep your "wheels rotating forward," you will find this stage of your life as Generative as I have.

Good luck and Godspeed, fellow pilgrim. I hope we will meet each other on the Generative path this stage of life offers and tell each other our stories.

Namaste

James (Jay) E. Hughes, Jr.

Aspen, Colorado 2012

---

[1] You can explore Jay's thinking on family and wealth further in his two books, *Family Wealth: Keeping it in the Family* and *Family: The Compact Among Generations*, or on his website at www.jamesehughes.com.

Introduction: Where to Begin?

Demographics don't lie. If your birthdate falls between January 1, 1946, and December 31, 1964, you are a baby boomer. Everywhere you look the headlines scream "boomers nearing retirement." Given the fact that financial markets have been on a roller-coaster ride over the last 10 years, financial security remains a hot topic. Who can afford to retire? Ads touting age-reducing plastic surgery are cropping up everywhere. Botox, anyone? Everyone, from gurus to academics, has advice for you on how to age gracefully. You might live to be 100. There's a lot to think about.

Yet there is rising acknowledgment of a new phenomenon, sometimes called an encore, the third act, prime time, or a second chapter. It now seems baby boomers are finding that the secret to retirement is not to do it, at least not in the conventional sense. Rather, they are seeking ways to take the experience, skills, and knowledge gleaned throughout their past and apply them on behalf of the people, places, and causes they care the most about today. For those who have been successful, and particularly those who have risen to leadership, this presents a unique opportunity.

We think it's time to take this phenomenon a step further, and that's what we are here to talk about.

Could This Be You?

Where are you today? Let us guess—50+ years old, proud of your accomplishments with good reason. You have spent your life thus far making a difference in all the ways you can. You have been a leader, a partner, a spouse, a mentor, a parent, and a friend. It's been great. You are blessed with few regrets and many satisfactions.

But now you feel it's time to do some serious thinking about the years ahead. Although you hate to admit it, you're not getting any younger, and it's starting to show. Things were supposed to get easier as you aged, but somehow it's not turning out that way.

The simple, more linear life trajectories we saw with our parents' generation are eluding us. Our lives are decidedly not simple. Perhaps those parents are still alive and need our help. Maybe our children have returned home because (pick one) they can't get jobs . . . a divorce is brewing . . . they can't afford a down payment . . .

And things are not any easier in your work life, either. The economic environment is getting crazier. Competition is cropping up everywhere. Perhaps the work itself just doesn't seem as fulfilling. You might even be getting a little bit bored. You have loved the success . . . but some days you just don't feel like going in; it's hard to find the same intensity you used to have every single day.

Or it could be the plain reality of aging with the attendant physical changes. Maybe you are tired. But you know it's more than that. There is restlessness and a yearning. As you look back and then look forward, you just don't see the productive years of your life as being over. You have more to do, more to learn, and more to give. When someone asks you when you are going to retire, you panic. The R word? Oh, that's not me, I want more than that. But what *do* you want?

And if you are the acknowledged leader in your business, your community, your profession, or your family, your difficulties multiply. It's hard to know whom to talk to. Everyone expects so much from you. Yet you know change is coming. You can hear the drumbeats. It's inevitable. And you'd rather do it right if you have to do it at all.

Doing it right is why we are here. Let us introduce ourselves. We are Kaycee Krysty, president emerita and Robert Moser (a.k.a. Bob), CEO of Laird Norton Tyee, a wealth management firm in Seattle, Washington. You can check out our bios in the back of the book. As we will explain as we go along, we have both built our careers on helping successful people deal with life's transitions. We have seen it all. And it goes without saying that we have hands-on experience—up close and personal—with transitions in our own lives. We've learned a lot along the way, and we plan to share it.

Intense? Me? Really? Yes, You

Here's some of what we know.

The realities of a lifetime of success are legion, but not all pretty. When you are at the top the buck stops with you, you are the final arbiter, and there is no real place to hide when mistakes are made. Yet you have loved every minute of it. So as change approaches the stakes for you are particularly high.

As a leader you may have tended to define yourself by your work. You have found your work to be creative and fulfilling. You have many personal relationships centered on your work. In social settings perhaps you are most comfortable when asked about your work and what you do. You work a lot, but it is more than working. Your work provides meaning and fulfillment in a way no other activity ever has. You enjoy it. You are immersed in the work, and your worldview is colored by what you do.

Our culture enables you in this focus on work. Others define you by your work as well. The most common question when you meet someone new is "What do you do?" not "What good book have you read lately?" Even friends and family may tend to see you in the box you've created for yourself by virtue of your success.

If you're honest with yourself you might admit that, although you may have many meaningful relationships outside of work, you have had to work very hard at cultivating them. If you've achieved both a successful marriage and a successful career, you've beaten the odds—although it is still likely that your spouse has either made some serious sacrifices to support you, or created a very independent life of his or her own, or perhaps both. Or perhaps marital success has eluded you altogether.

Psychologists call this style "work intensive." It's not a pathology, it's just a description of a certain way some people—most successful people—live their lives. Bob and Kaycee both admit to a work-intensive style. If you are honest you probably will admit the same. So how can somebody like us possibly have a life after work?

This way of being is common to many executives and professionals, but those at the very top may take it a step further. As a leader, particularly amid times of extraordinary growth or turmoil, you become intertwined with your organization in deeply personal ways. You carry the weight of it all on your shoulders. All of this increases the angst that you face when transition is on the horizon.

Now, It's Your Turn

One of the least understood challenges of leadership is the difficulty you as a leader face when managing your own life. We are not talking about merely finding balance in your life. (Kaycee and Bob would argue that balance is overrated anyway.) Rather, it's about how you deal with change. When you are a leader, helping others deal with change is the essence of your job. So you must be good at handling change, right? Somehow, though, when it comes to your personal life, all bets seem to be off. Whether the change is thrust upon you or you choose it doesn't seem to matter; it is still more difficult because the change is your own.

Leaders are human too—we have health crises and identity crises just like anyone else. And for those of us in the baby boom generation the inevitable drumbeat of our aging is upon us. When you are a leader you're not likely to garner quite as much sympathy for your problems. You are alpha dog, after all, top of the heap. Can't you just retire and (fill in the blank) play golf . . . fly fish . . . twiddle your thumbs . . . with no worries? Isn't that what we all are supposed to have been working so hard for—*not* having to work? Yet somewhere in your heart of hearts there is a little voice screaming "NO! I'm not done yet!" And there you sit.

In every other area of your life you are a prime mover. People look to you to get things done. But on this matter, what you do with your own future, you resemble some kind of critter in the headlights. Thank goodness no one has noticed; at least you *hope* no one has.

Standing on the Edge of the Cliff

It's a risky business, this. As a leader, once you even drop a hint that you might be moving on, people around you naturally divide into two categories: some whose vested interest is in keeping you in place, and others who want you gone.

If your head is not clear on the matter, you risk damaging the organization you have probably invested your heart and soul in. And it is unlikely your head is clear when you haven't given yourself any time to think about it!

The coming retirement of so many baby boom business leaders has crisis potential written all over it. Many organizations give lip service to having a succession plan, but in reality what they have is a hit-by-the-bus plan. Every consultant recommends such a plan; it's in their word-processing system. Leaders are often charged by their boards to groom successors, but that seldom goes very deep. Yet succession is just not happening.

The chief obstacle for most leaders at this point is the very thing that has taken them to the top: intensity. (That's why they call us "work intensives.") We can speak from our own experience when we say that our personal identities have been closely linked to our work. We love working. Both of us have experienced difficulty separating work from life and have tended to see much if not most of the world through the lens our lifetime of work has given us. It's fair to say that for people like us, work has provided great personal satisfaction. No wonder it's so difficult to look beyond it.

Yet look beyond it we must. It's time to create a new definition for retirement. A definition that is not about pulling away but about plunging in, about creating a way to extend leadership throughout your lifetime, a definition that embraces the passion and intensity of the past and brings it forward to impact the things that matter most.

Now, having worked together to make Kaycee's transition a success, and having worked with many others in similar circumstances over the past 20 years, we can say with some certainty that there is hope. It's not easy, it certainly requires work, and it may require you to do some things that are out of character or uncomfortable (like putting yourself first). But it is eminently doable. The outcome can be amazing, allowing you to experience a lifetime of leadership rather than an end to your leadership. And the world needs leaders. You. That's why we have written this book.

PART I

Redefining Retirement

CHAPTER 1

It's All about You (Really It Is)

If you have lived your life as a leader, you might be surprised at the kinds of things that get in your way at this point in your life. As you face the road ahead, you may find that some of the very things that fueled your success are now roadblocks. It will take some careful thought to clear the road, and perhaps a willingness to consider alternative routes.

We versus Me

Most of us learned early in our business careers the power of *we* versus the power of *me*. You know that at the beginning of your career you were prized as an employee based on individual achievement—but what took you up the ladder was an ability to unite people as teams to get important work done. And the higher you flew, the more essential you found the power of *we*, and the more destructive you found too much *me*.

So herein lies the paradox—after a long career of the *we*, you cannot create and embrace your own transition without moving back to the *me*. It may feel like an unnatural act, but you have to do it. The reality is this: *Traditional business succession planning has it in the wrong order.* In almost every case the planning process begins with a focus on the business or organization, and it usually gets derailed right there. To get it right, you as a leader need to first figure out your own future. Then with your own plan in place, you can work with key stakeholders to plan for your organization. Forget grooming your successor; you need to groom yourself first.

In fact, our experience suggests that not putting yourself first takes the success out of succession. Think about it. How many leaders have you seen clinging to their organization on the mistaken belief that it could not survive without them? Come on, we all know that if you have done your job well you have great people in place to carry on. The real measure of your success may be your own "dispense-ability."

How many leaders do you know whose health or board of directors forced their transition, yet they cannot bring themselves to leave the organization alone? We call this the Brett Favre syndrome (more about this later), but it is no joke. There are clear examples throughout business and public life of those who have their identity so tied up in their leadership role that they can't recognize when it's time to move on.

It's Time for It to Be All about You

If you're reading this book you probably haven't gone down the Favre road—appearing ridiculous to everyone but yourself—but you are worried that you might. Or you have had some sort of wake-up call—health, business issues, family matters, whatever. You know that as the leader no one is likely to hold up a mirror. Come on, who ever says "it's time for you to move on" to their boss? What is the bottom line? You have to do it yourself.

This could be the act of ultimate leadership—figuring out how to move out and onward to open the field for the success of others. Our observations suggest that when you as a leader have determined your own destination, you allow what is right for the organization to emerge naturally.

So this book is about creating your own strategy for what's next. It's not about traditional retirement planning—although it contains some similar elements—because traditional retirement doesn't work for leaders like you. Seriously, how many apocryphal stories have you heard in which a former CEO dies six months after retiring to the desert for golf? Instead, we are talking about creating something more.

What works for people like us is having a plan to do something meaningful and leave a legacy. In short, you need to continue somehow, some way, in being the person you are, a leader.

And you'll be happy to note that this isn't rocket science. Most of what you need to know you is already in your arsenal. You already tackled very similar tasks at some point in your career. This will be about using your skills on a new strategic planning project, yourself.

Real Life, Real Money

Is this about money? Yes, your financial resources have a significant role to play. It's hard to be creative with your life if you don't have some sense of financial peace of mind. As in your business life, a long-range strategy and the discipline to execute on it are keys to financial sustainability.

But you want to go beyond just analyzing the dollars and cents. The lessons we have learned from the business leaders and the families that we serve is that there are truly two sides to a balance sheet. Not just assets and liabilities, mind you, but human and financial capital. Your real wealth is measured not just in dollars but also in these human terms, the wealth of health, relationships, and purpose. We call this your *human capital.* You will be hearing a lot about it.

So it is about the money at some level, but so much more. At the end of the day, success will be measured not by how much you had but by what you did. Leveraging both your human capital and financial capital is the task. We suggest that failure to do so should not be an option.

Wealth Regeneration, What's That?

When asked what we do, we find we are often dispelling myths. "You manage people's money, right?" "No," we answer, "We manage their *wealth*, in fact, we help them *regenerate* it." The discipline we call Wealth Regeneration is both an art and a science. The purpose of Wealth Regeneration is to weave together all aspects of wealth—human capital and financial capital—to promote desired outcomes throughout lifetimes and across generations. It is a strategic approach ideally suited to the challenges leaders face when they consider retirement.

Wealth Regeneration is unique. It is a practice born out of the collective wisdom of our company's founders, the Laird Norton family—seven generations strong and thriving—coupled with new lessons we have learned serving emerging wealth creators in the Pacific Northwest. Our goal is to share its secrets with you.

Old Money

Our founders, the Laird Norton family, have achieved something very few families in America have achieved—a flourishing family and financial success, now seven generations strong.

There are many factors that have contributed to this achievement, but one thing stands clear. Throughout its history, the Laird Norton family has tended its human capital with as much care as its financial capital. As a result, when faced with change, whether economic or societal, this family always found a way to manage the change. The Laird Norton family's precious human capital has provided the resilience to weather both good times and crises for more than 150 years.

You cannot always expect that kind of result from financial capital, no matter how well managed. Sometimes human capital is the only thing that gets you through. So it is wise to take care of it.

New Wealth

Our work with recent wealth creators offers another kind of insight. Over the last 20 years there's been an amazing boom in entrepreneurship. It seems more new fortunes have been created than at any time since the Gilded Age. The hallmark of this new wave of wealth creators is not what you might expect, technology or innovation; rather, it is *adaptation.* Particularly the kind of adaptation that looks at various elements that already exist and imagines them functioning in new ways. And then creates the new way.

These entrepreneurs didn't invent the computer—they made it useful. Same thing with the Internet—they didn't create it, but they have made it a powerful tool for all of us. And all across many traditional businesses the same phenomenon has occurred. Existing elements are combined in bold new ways, creating even more value and growth.

The dictionary definition of adaptation is "adjustment to environmental conditions." We use the word in its practical sense. It describes the process of bringing seemingly disparate elements together in new ways to solve new problems. In the changing times we live in, this kind of adaptation is crucial to success by any measure.

Adaptation is by its very nature pragmatic and forward looking. It is clearly the best strategic posture in times of change. And the one thing you can count on is change! Change is ongoing; it never stops. The most successful of the new wealth creators—those who succeed in both business and personal life—have made adaptation a part of who they are, not just what they do. They use their adaptive mindset to fully embrace change wherever they find it and meet it head on. You can, too.

The Principles

Here are the key principles of Wealth Regeneration:

• Tend to your financial capital *very* well (we are financial people, after all).
• Mind your human capital with at least as much fervor as you tend to your financial capital (or maybe more).
• Stay open to adaptation in the face of change (because you never know).

With Wealth Regeneration you follow these principles to work with intention toward the future you desire. It's that straightforward, although we won't say it's simple. And as we've said before, these principles work particularly well when you are right in the midst of change. Fundamentally that's all retirement is, a change, albeit a profound one. It makes sense to be considering it with care.

What's Next?

You are not alone. It's well recognized that human life happens in phases. Historically the most attention has been paid to life phases in the early years, such as adolescents and the terrible twos. But as baby boomers begin to hit 65, you are hearing more and more about another stage. Some call it the third chapter; others call it a second act or an encore. Whatever you call it, the notion of staying vibrant, connected, and relevant as we age has great appeal. We all want lives of meaning.

As we see it, the pressure created by the increasing complexity of life combined with this desire for meaning makes the case for Wealth Regeneration very compelling. Now more than ever, careful stewardship of both your human capital and financial capital while readily adapting in the face of change will be needed at every twist and turn in the road ahead.

You Have to Sleep at Night

You might be surprised that we have not yet talked much about money. What we know from experience is this: When change is afoot, a serious chicken and egg problem arises when it comes to your life and your money. Here's the thing. It is almost impossible to figure out what's next in life if you don't have a clear sense of your finances. And it's also true that what's next could affect those finances, perhaps in ways that are difficult to predict. This is what makes traditional linear retirement planning no longer relevant for our times.

Take this example: You don't think you're ready to quit totally, but you know it's time for you to step down. What do you figure out first? What you want to be doing? How you might stay employed? Or how much money will you need? Done right, the process is one of iterations, going back and forth and measuring trade-offs. And those iterations don't end when a decision is made and acted upon. Because as soon as you've made a decision, something else changes and you are back at it again.

Another example—you have recently retired but find yourself restless. You will probably go back to work some way, somehow, but you would like to explore something different. Someone suggests that you take a "gap year" where you move to a new location and undertake things completely unrelated to your former life. How could that work? And what if that leads you to a completely new set of choices?

Old-style planning offered a road map, a guide along a predetermined route. Now, there is nothing wrong with a road map—just as long as you never stray off course, run out of gas, or change your mind about where you're going. For the constantly changing future we all face, a new instrument is needed—something more like a GPS—so when change happens (and it will), you are ready to "recalculate route," as the comforting voice might say.

That's how to think about Wealth Regeneration, as a trusted companion for the road ahead. It's a way of putting a process in place for yourself that "recalculates route." And it helps you do so in a thoughtful and consistent way whenever the times, economics, minds, or health may change. And they will change.

PARTING THOUGHTS

1. When was the last time you intentionally tended your human capital?
2. What does peace of mind mean to you?
3. How do you practice adaptation in your personal life?

CHAPTER 2

The "R" Word

It may happen again today—another meeting with another soon-to-be-former CEO, who when asked about what's next, gives a strained shrug. "I don't know," he says. "I am sure something will turn up. I'm just focused on the business." We have seen it time after time. You can change that CEO title for any other high-level job—community leader, chief surgeon, managing director, or "of counsel," to name a few possibilities. But in every case when retirement is on the horizon, the answer is pretty much the same. These high-powered individuals are on the brink of substantial life changes and at a loss as to what to do next.

In many cases these are folks who have much of their identity tied up in what they do. Throughout their adult lives their primary energy and focus has been on their occupation. Whether it's founding a business, leading a team, or devising a breakthrough medical technique, getting things done is the air they breathe. And it is the lens through which they see the world. Can you relate?

For those of us with what are called "work-intensive personalities," the thought of not working is an unsettling one indeed. While we certainly love our families, friends, and community, they have not necessarily been the most significant sources of our life satisfaction. Although we may be loath to admit it, often work has. For that reason, traditional retirement is not only unattractive, it may be out-and-out impossible. What in heaven's name would we do with ourselves?

How do we know? Well, because Bob and Kaycee are both "one of those people." Perhaps you are too. Or perhaps you are married to one. In our case, we have spent our careers helping other successful people achieve and maintain long-term financial success, and we have been very good at it. Yet we still found much to learn when it came to "what's next" in our own lives.

There Are Lots of Us

We have written about this topic at this time because of the huge wave of baby boomers cascading toward later life. We believe that embedded in the boomer tsunami is a large coterie of people just like us who aren't ready to let go. If you're reading this, we suspect you may feel the same way. We are folks just like you who have worked passionately at our professions all our lives and can't envision having it any other way. We like to think that the skills, energy, experience, and knowledge capital that took us to the top are needed more than ever in the world ahead. So how can we just stop?

As we think about that CEO who announces "something will turn up," we suspect he already knows and fears the answer. All of us "work intensives" know in our gut that the answer is not pretty. The stories we hear about others are shared quietly among like-minded friends. Without finding a new direction in life, what shows up at retirement for hard chargers is simple: death, disability, divorce, or decline. No thank you.

Now What?

The question of what to do next is, on first blush, a human issue, yet we find it is also a resource question. While financial security won't answer the "what to do" question, you will find that the question is even more difficult to answer without a solid financial strategy in place. At its core, solving this dilemma is about peace of mind. How can you possibly consider what you might do next if you have no idea of the financial implications?

We have found that in the best outcomes, human and financial matters become positively intertwined. This means that the human supports the financial as the financial supports (and ideally) leverages the human. Ask yourself, what did you make all this money for, if it was not to make life better for yourself and those you love?

So let's get back to our "work intensive" for a moment. We are making an assumption here. Working at the top tier of your business or profession over a period of years usually results in financial rewards. With a bit of discipline you may have put together a decent financial position, perhaps in spite of the recent economic difficulties. If you're like most people, though, you will find it a challenge to translate that position into choices. How much is enough? What can I really do with what I have? These are things you need to know in order to pursue what's next.

Yet it will still boil down to figuring out what it is you really want to do and why. Finding the answer means going deeper than just whether or not you can cover monthly expenses. Once you have set your course, sorting out the money is relatively easy. So what do you want?

The Hero's Farewell

We find it's always instructive to understand what others have done. Jeffrey Sonnenfeld, a professor at the Yale School of Management and founder of the nonprofit Chief Executive Leadership Institute, has written the classic book on transition for those at the top. Published in the 1980s, his analysis and research has stood the test of time. *The Hero's Farewell* remains the go-to book for anyone seriously interested in the impact of business succession on the organization's leader. Sonnenfeld really got it right, and he got it right the first time.

In doing his research he interviewed over 100 CEOs and soon-to-be-retired CEOs about their experiences. He was not surprised to find that they didn't *like* to use the word "retirement" in conversation. In fact, he was often careful to couch his research in terms of business succession just so he could get his targets to agree to be interviewed at all. But the questions he asked were very much to the point about the realities and possibilities of retirement. In fact, his lead question was, "What has been the most rejuvenating aspect of your retirement?"

As Sonnenfeld analyzed his data, he found clear patterns emerging. The CEOs began to fall into one of four categories, which he labeled Monarchs, Generals, Governors, and Ambassadors. Not only does this taxonomy remain relevant for understanding transition at the CEO level, but we find it works just as well for anyone whose career has been a major source of personal identity. More about that in a minute.

Here is Sonnenfeld's description of the leaders' departure styles:

Monarchs do not leave office until they are decisively forced out through the death of the chief executive or through a . . . palace revolt. . . .

Generals depart in a style also marked by forcible exit. Here the chief executive leaves office reluctantly, but plots his return and quickly comes back to office out of retirement in order to rescue the company from the real or imagined inadequacy of his or her successor.

Ambassadors, by contrast, leave office quite gracefully and frequently served as postretirement mentors. They may remain on the Board of Directors for some time, but they do not try to sabotage the successor. . . .

Finally, *Governors* rule for a limited term of office then shift to other vocational outlets entirely after retirement.[1]

We know people who fit each of these categories and we bet you do, too. Did you find that thoughts of some of the leaders you have known came to mind when you read the descriptions? And it is clearly not just CEOs whom this taxonomy fits.

We see these archetypes displayed in our wider culture. Brett Favre can only be described as a general scrambling and fighting to stay on top. Tony Bennett—at least until recently—seemed a natural monarch, gracefully carrying forward a storied career. And what about Betty White? Steve Martin is a clear governor moving from success as a comedian and actor to writing acclaimed novels and now a music career. Ambassador examples abound. Jimmy Carter comes to mind as someone who continued on after his presidency to use his political skills and relationships in positive ways, making himself available to his successors, ultimately resulting in a Nobel Prize. Colin Powell is quite literally someone who went from the status of general to ambassador. And the list goes on.

What about Me?

But how does this work for us regular people? The reality is that most monarchs are not like Tony Bennett; they can't continue to gracefully age in place pursuing exactly the same career until the end of life. Case in point—think surgeons, airline pilots, trial attorneys; sometimes age just wins.

Brett Favre may be the archetype general, fighting to keep the position that is quickly slipping from his grasp. The challenge for generals is to recognize who they are. Many, perhaps most, do not and—as is the case with Favre—can appear ridiculous, even though rarely told that to their face. Each of us has known someone in that predicament. If only they could see themselves as others see them.

Yet there's hope. The choice is *not* just retire and go sit and do nothing. Both the ambassador style and the governor style hold out models that give those of us for whom traditional retirement is not appealing an alternative

---

[1] Sonnenfeld, Jeffrey. *The Hero's Farewell: What Happens When CEOs Retire* (New York: Oxford University Press, Inc., 1988), 70–71.

vision for the future. The challenge is figuring it out. And here's the scary part—this is about you, not a celebrity. What does this mean for you?

For all of us whose professional lives have been a major part of who we are, the prospect of an exit strategy may be less than thrilling. We love what we do, we see ourselves still contributing, and we may be secretly grateful that the recent economic downturn gives us the cover we need to avoid addressing the issue at all. But the reality of aging comes creeping back to haunt us. Some days we just must look this in the face.

What We've Learned

We have spent the past several years talking to many individuals right in the vortex of transition. Some have successfully made it to the other side; others stand on the brink gearing up for the plunge. But we must say, in all cases the validity of Sonnenfeld's taxonomy remains. Whether monarchs, generals, ambassadors, or governors, the patterns he studied and documented are alive and well today for all of us baby boomers

We have spoken to monarchs who fully intend to die with their boots on. We have spoken to generals who are off the field of engagement but are waiting, wishing, and hoping their value will be recognized and they will be called back to relive old glories. And we have spoken to those who would be classified as governors and ambassadors—those who have moved on, found ways to embrace change, and continue to live lives that have meaning and purpose, passion and productivity.

Here are some of our key observations:

- Most begin their journey in the monarch or general mode (it's simple human nature to ignore or resist the fact of inevitable change).
- The willingness to consider alternatives is most often triggered by some life situation that grabs our attention, like health or business change.
- Those that did find their way to a governor or ambassador solution spent time and energy on self-reflection, as uncomfortable as that may seem.
- The path to transition is often not immediately apparent. It takes work and sometimes experimentation to uncover (some of the best lessons emerge from mistakes made).
- A strategy for financial security is always part of the solution. It's difficult to make any kind of change when you feel at risk.
- Focusing on financial security alone without addressing the human issues always fails.

There is much to reflect upon here.

When faced with planning for the future, the first thing most of us do is begin with an inventory of our financial assets. It is practically a knee-jerk reaction. We are not saying financial resources are not important; they most certainly are. Only that addressing financial assets without looking at the human side provides an unbalanced and incomplete picture. Another kind of inventory is needed—an inventory that looks at all aspects of your wealth. We'd be surprised if you told us that your money is your most prized possession. Wealth is so much more than that. That's what you need to be thinking about if you want to find your way.

Where Do You Fit?

It can be helpful too to consider where you might fit in Sonnenfeld's taxonomy. Do you know whether you are a general or a monarch? Will you seek to be an ambassador or a governor? You will find it is possible to be a moving target!

We think of this world as a grid (see Figure 2.1).

FIGURE 2.1 Departure Style Grid

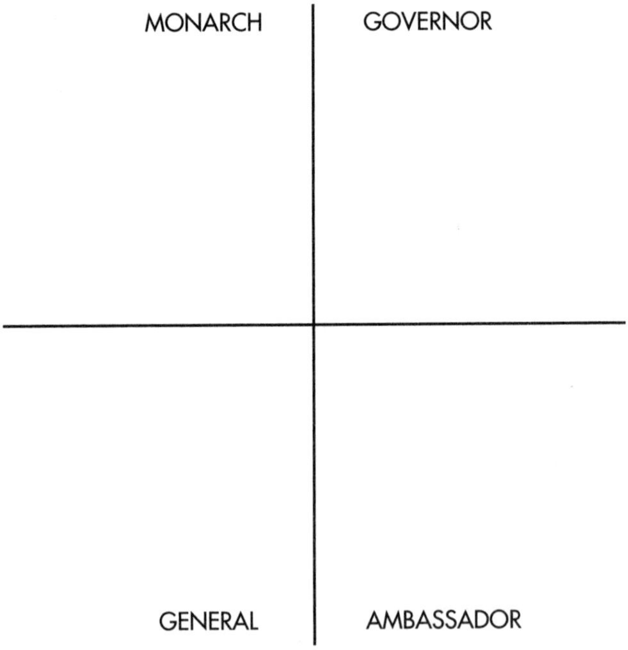

MONARCH   GOVERNOR

GENERAL   AMBASSADOR

At any one time it is likely you have some elements of all four styles, but one style tends to predominate. The challenge is in understanding where you are and making choices to move to a new position on the grid. You can actually plot where you are, if you can be honest enough with yourself to assess it.

Kaycee will now readily admit she began her transition as a hard-core monarch. That is, until serious health issues—not once but twice—caught her attention and made her question that assumption. She found it a difficult road to move to true ambassador status, with many twists and turns along the way, as Bob can attest (see Figure 2.2). But she made it.

Her story mirrors that of so many others, first seeing themselves as invincible, and then facing life's reality.

Or perhaps you think you are a monarch and should stay that way—but tomorrow your board of directors stages a palace coup. Or a buyer comes along for the business offering a price that can't be turned down in good conscience. In either case you will be moving out. So here are your choices: Do you move to general mode, wishing and hoping they will need you again? Or maybe just wait out your covenant not to compete so you can start

FIGURE 2.2   Kaycee's Journey

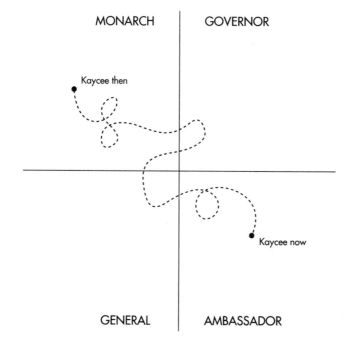

FIGURE 2.3 What Will Your Journey Look Like?

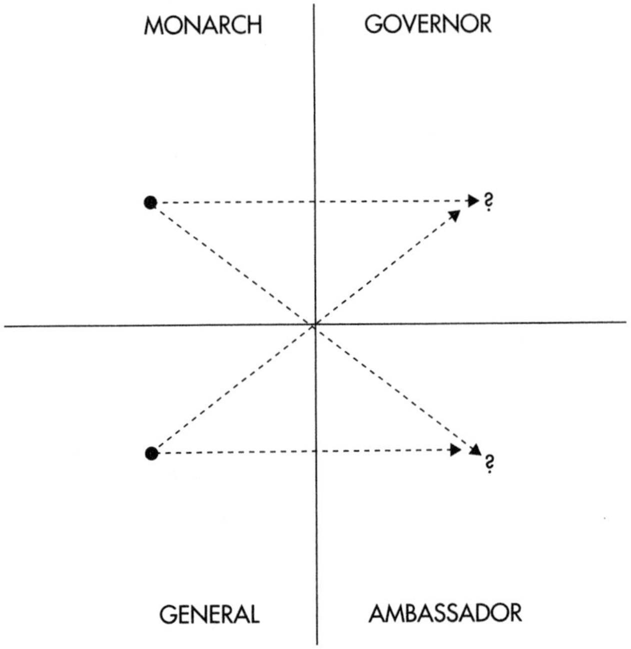

all over again? Or do you move on? And please note this quandary is not about the money, it's about what you are going to do with your life.

Even for those wise enough to recognize that monarch status is rarely sustainable and general status rarely satisfying, finding a way to move to the right side of the quadrant is daunting (see Figure 2.3). It requires essentially redefining who you are, and that, as they say, is one tall order.

No matter how you look at it, you still have to decide what road to take.

We are here to help. Is this about human potential? Or is this about finance? Well, quite honestly, it's both. Let's let Wealth Regeneration guide you along the way.

PARTING THOUGHTS

1. What do you fear most about retirement?
2. Are you a governor, a monarch, a general, or an ambassador?
3. What do you do to balance your work-intensive style?

CHAPTER 3

The Grab Bag of Life

Perhaps the biggest obstacle to figuring out what's next on your horizon is the essential nature of our lives today. It's about change, and if we were to paraphrase the famous catchphrase of the Clinton campaign, we'd say— it's about change, stupid! Change is everywhere. The good news is that we are all already smart enough to know that. Now it's down to what to do about it.

Change Has Impact

Change in and of itself is not a bad thing. We know it comes in at least three forms—change you choose, change that is inevitable, and change that occurs unexpectedly because of a somewhat random event. For example, retirement can happen for any of these reasons. You could:

- Decide enough is enough so "I'm out of here", or
- Reach a mandatory retirement age, or
- Experience a health issue that precludes your continuing to work.

Any of these things could happen. These are some of the most obvious changes that fuel someone's choice to retire; of course there are many more possibilities. Yet it's more than that. The real pace of change in your life is measured in multiple ways, change piled upon change. It's never just about work. Have your kids moved home because they can't get jobs? Does your aging parent need you? Is the occupation you have loved for so many years one of those slated for demise by technological leaps? Are you just bored?

Some of the changes you experience may not seem to be such a big deal. Except that it adds up. Perhaps the local hardware store you relied on for advice for many years had to close when the big-box store opened down the street. Or it could be as simple as your dentist of many years moving away. And even if it's change for the better, the sheer volume of change in today's world can be daunting.

We find one of the most interesting aspects of dealing with change is how subtle its impact can be. You have to think about it to recognize it. And it is often accretive. The experience of change can be incredibly pervasive. What all of us know, whether or not we admit it, is that change is the new normal. And rapid change to boot. You must find ways to embrace it, if you don't want it to wear you down.

Managing Change

As someone who has leadership experience, at some point in your career you have undoubtedly had to manage through changes—mergers, downsizings, strategic realignments, re-engineerings—as they are euphemistically called. In the business world managing change has become something of a science with its own body of literature and research. Some would argue that real leadership is all about managing change. Yet at its heart managing change is a fundamentally human issue.

In managing any big project you ask yourself: How do I get these people through to the other side? You know that human beings fundamentally and systematically avoid change. You also know from experience that it takes time and startling amounts of willpower to make change that is lasting. And it's not just big changes that are problematical either—moving someone to a new cubicle can produce just as much fallout as assigning him or her a new job description. (We might argue that the new job description is easier!) Messy work, this.

We humans hate change; we will avoid it at every turn in ways both subtle and perverse. And then we will look ourselves right in the eye and proclaim we really are on board with the changes. Not. You've been there and you've seen it. So don't kid yourself about what change will mean when it's personal.

As you look to your own situation it is tempting to believe that because it is your life we are talking about (where you are theoretically completely in charge), dealing with change will be easier. Nothing could be further from the truth. When it comes to your own life, it takes every skill you have developed leading others plus a willingness to engage in an uncomfortable level of honesty with your own toughest critic (you) to lead yourself forward. Whew!

The New Rules

In their book *LifeLaunch*, authors Pamela McLean and Frederic Hudson lay out what they see as new rules for dealing with life in the face of accelerating change. McLean and Hudson are widely acknowledged as pioneers in the life coaching movement through their training organization, the Hudson Institute of Santa Barbara. Their approach is thoughtful and provocative and based on many years of work with individuals seeking to relaunch their lives.

What McLean and Hudson propose is a simple but elegant comparison about how life's rules have changed over the centuries. We find their way of looking at this to be a useful perspective in how you consider change—particularly a major change in your own life, like retirement.

McLean and Hudson argue that the pace of change in human life is increasing exponentially. No surprise there. They first look at the history of how humans have successfully lived lives using static and linear expectations. They call these the old rules. These are the rules that society expected good girls and boys to play by if they wanted to win. As McLean and Hudson point out, these rules just don't work anymore. They then pose new rules, ways of addressing change that are circular, not linear, much more in line with the way we live our lives today.

So here are their rules both new and old:

Then—The Linear Rule

This rule promised rewards for those who worked hard, played fair, and colored between the lines. You could expect things to get better and better. Maybe that worked a generation ago, but certainly not now.

Now—The Circular Rule

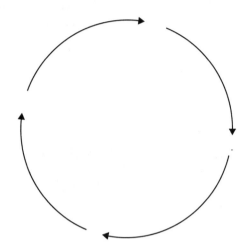

Life has seasons; sometimes it's good and sometimes it's difficult. As McLean and Hudson point out, your life is in constant change and "for the most part, it doesn't get better or worse, it just gets different."

Then—The Outside-In Rule

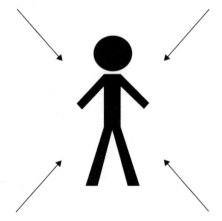

It used to be that the boundaries of your life were circumscribed by external institutions—family, church, community, and work. You knew what to do in life because these entities prescribed it for you.

Now—The Inside-Out Rule

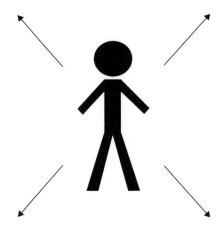

These external agencies no longer provide a secure way of being, a road map for success. Perhaps their worldview is no longer relevant because of changing times, or perhaps their perspective just does not work for you anymore. In either case the new rule suggests that dealing with change comes from your own firm internal anchor.

Then—The Learning-Is-for-Kids Rule

It's clear that throughout history learning has been for the young. Grownups took what had been learned in their early years and just got to work making life work. Why would adults want to keep learning? Who had time? What difference would it make?

Now—The Learning-Is-Lifelong Rule

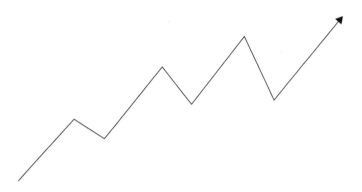

In changing times there is no doubt that learning new things is both the best offense and the best defense. Those who keep on learning—whether it's about values or technical skills, knowledge or human behavior—are more likely to thrive, whatever the challenge of change.

Then—The Steady-State Rule

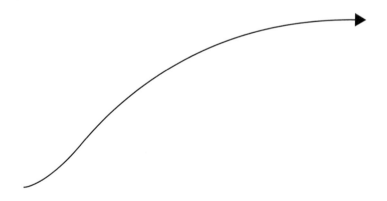

McLean and Hudson's last rule cuts to the heart of our Wealth Regeneration principles. Under this old rule we made assumptions about how life would turn out. If we had followed all the other old rules, we could expect to reach a point in life of stability and security, a place where things would only get better. That's what we were working for. (We're not sure this rule was ever true, but people certainly believed in it, hence traditional retirement planning.)

Now—The Continuous Change Rule

Everything changes, all the time. Just when you think you have things figured out, you discover you don't. That's today's reality. The trick is embracing it all. McLean and Hudson say it well: "If you can connect to what is of lasting worth, while learning new directions to explore, you can thrive on change." That is why the ability to adapt to change is key.[1]

If McLean and Hudson's rules don't convince you that change is all around us, just give yourself the opportunity to look back over the last five years of your own life. What changes have you seen that you never expected to see? Like many aging parents, our own parents would often talk about all the things they had been amazed to see over their lifetimes—the end of the Second World War, television, the Berlin wall coming down—you get the picture. Well, if you apply the same logic to merely the last five years of your own life you will see how quickly things are moving—it's faster and faster. The trick is not to let it make you dizzy but rather to grab on and go along for the ride.

Wealth Regeneration is designed to help you do this in your own way, as a leader within your life. The discipline of Wealth Regeneration provides effective tools to grasp, seize, and embrace the changes that are before you, to adapt, and to be able to handily "recalculate the route" on the road you have chosen. Because change is coming; it is the only thing you can count on.

PARTING THOUGHTS ────────────────

1. What lessons have you learned throughout your career about dealing with change?
2. Is there a change on the horizon that is prompting you to plan today?
3. Are there other rules about change that you see out there?

---

[1] Our thanks to the Hudson Institute for allowing us to present these concepts from their book: *LifeLaunch: A Passionate Guide to the Rest of Your Life*, by Pamela McLean and Frederic Hudson (Santa Barbara: The Hudson Institute Press, 1995).

CHAPTER 4

It's Not Rocket Science

No question about it, you need a plan, a strategy, and some discipline to face what's ahead. We have good news. We're here to tell you that you are already master or mistress of the key techniques needed to create such a plan, and you may not even be aware of it. Everything you need to know you already learned in business school—or the school of hard knocks. The difference is learning how to apply it to your personal life. We see this with almost every business, professional, or community leader we work with: great skills that just need to be reoriented toward personal life.

The skills we suspect you probably already have in your arsenal include strategic planning, change management, financial forecasting, risk assessment, building teams, and holding people accountable. It's unlikely you've accomplished all that you have in life without these skills among many others. And we will add one more to the essential list: an understanding of the importance of meaningful work, both for you and those you care for.

Strategic Planning

The most fundamental skill needed here is strategic planning. At the end of the day that's what is crucial for framing your decisions about what's next. No one gets to the top without mastering that skill, and you didn't either. Even if you present yourself as a skeptic to the planning folderol that many companies engage in ("I hate retreats" or "I don't do that vision thing"), you know that *organizations with a clear purpose outperform*.

Bob is a skeptic when it comes to a lot of the strategic planning rituals. Kumbaya, anyone? It should be no surprise that Kaycee is a huge fan of it. But on this we both agree—well-conceived strategy creates success.

Your personal life is no different.

We want you to give yourself the time and space to uncover and articulate your own individual mission, vision, purpose, and values. We don't care what you call them; they are the linchpin of Wealth Regeneration. Remember the famous quote from the Cheshire Cat in *Alice in Wonderland*?

Alice:	Would you tell me, please, which way I ought to go from here?
The Cheshire Cat:	That depends a good deal on where you want to get to.
Alice:	I don't much care where.
The Cheshire Cat:	Then it doesn't much matter which way you go.
Alice:	. . . So long as I get somewhere.
The Cheshire Cat:	Oh, you're sure to do that, if only you walk long enough.

Lewis Carroll, *Alice In Wonderland*

Our view is that at this point in your life just getting somewhere is not good enough. It needs to be the place you would actually like to go. That's why the strategy part of this exercise—or mission, vision, purpose, or whatever you want to call it—is so important. You want to avoid, as the Cat pointed out, the prospect of a long and aimless walk.

We also bet that that your years in the trenches have given you pretty good radar for the difference between the tactical and strategic. You can discern the difference between what to do and why you might choose to do it. You have had the experience of sweeping aside distracting tactics to focus on core strategy, and you've helped others do the same. You will definitely need that skill on the road ahead.

You will also find valuable your ability to cut to the chase, to boil ideas down to their essence. We are not going to suggest that you create a multipage plan, but we do know that getting key elements documented in some form increases success. Expect to write some things; just keep it short and sweet.

Change Management

Throughout your working life you've experienced change, over and over. Even those who stayed with the same organization for many years can look back over their experience and recognize the velocity of change. In a business setting, change is viewed as something to be managed, and to a great degree it can be. That's why we are always surprised when we see successful people who fail to manage change in their own lives.

Incorporating a more proactive approach to change, as is now recognized as best practice for business, makes more sense. The classic change model goes something like this:

- Look change in the eye—what is it? Is it by choice? By chance? Or from life's inevitabilities?
- Decide what you want to do about it—depending upon the nature of the change you are facing, you may have more or less control. But there are always choices. Make them.
- Gather the troops and tools—be sure all the necessary ingredients are in place, then get them rolling.
- Recognize the milestones along the way—all change is incremental. We move through change more easily when progress is noted.

You have probably worked with teams through times of change more than once in your career, using fundamentally this approach. So don't be surprised to find that it works in your own life just as well.

Financial Forecasting

No, you don't need to know how to do the actual forecasting itself. Whew! You can and probably should hire someone to do personal financial forecasts (more about that later). The skill you must have is *using* the forecasts. You need to know how to read and interpret forecasts, not how to create them. As in budget reviews and long-range business planning, the key is figuring out what makes the forecast tick. Here's what you probably already know how to do:

- Understand the assumptions—you want to be able to wrap your head around the underlying assumptions of the forecast. Often you can make a commonsense assessment that is just as valid as anything more scientific, if you just understand the assumptions.
- Find the sensitivities—there are always a few factors that, when changed, swing the forecast significantly. Others, not so much. What are those sensitivities? Are they things you can control?
- Test for risk—what are the downsides? Well, you can't focus only on the downside (or you just might hide under your desk!). But you need to know what it looks like. The resilience of the forecast can be determined by how much downside it can absorb before producing a completely unacceptable result.

You have undoubtedly done all these things when reviewing forecasts over the years. Now it's time to do them for the most interesting long-range plan of all, your own. We'll provide you with examples along the way.

Risk Assessment

Assessing risk is another key business skill notably underused and under-valued in personal life. Because there are never rewards without risk, knowing what risks to take and how to take them intelligently pays off.

Let us give you a concrete example of how smart business people fail to assess risk properly in their own lives: insurance deductibles. Time after time we still see highly successful people who pay much higher insurance premiums than they need to because they are more "comfortable" with a $500 deductible on their car insurance than the higher deductible that may make more sense. Remember, higher deductibles equal lower premiums. And to make matters worse, we often see this paired with inadequate liability coverage. Yet we all know that a large liability claim can be personally catastrophic, clearly more damaging than paying a few thousand dollars for car repairs.

In business you would never make trade-offs like this, so why would you do it personally?

When it comes to personal risk assessment there are certainly subtleties that differentiate it from business. Peace of mind, for example. It's more difficult to take risks when it's the kind of thing that keeps you up at night. Still, the essential elements of dealing with risk remain the same whether it's your personal business or commercial business. Here they are:

- Identify the risk,
- Quantify the risk, and
- Deal with it.

When you deal with risk, you will find there are basically only three choices. You can avoid risk altogether, take action to mitigate it, or find a way to share the risk with others.

We make these choices all the time in our everyday actions and don't even think about it. Bringing this unconscious risk assessment process into the open—making it an acknowledged part of your planning process—

yields all kinds of dividends. You'll think about risk more strategically, and you may find you are more comfortable taking risk.

Building Teams

Great teams drive great outcomes. In fact, we find it is rare to get a great outcome without a strong team to deliver it. You know this works, and you know how to build a team. Your own personal affairs will benefit from the team approach as well. You can build the strongest team possible in the same way you built teams over all the years of your career.

For your own personal team you'll find that the same principles apply. What you have always sought in team members are still the things you're looking for: skill, integrity, and ability to communicate, with perhaps a sense of humor? For this team you'll also want those whose style meshes with your personal work style: thinking on your feet, problem solving, and a quick study in complex situations. Remember, you intend to trust these folks with your own personal business. They should be top notch in all the ways that matter to you.

Typically your team will include your attorney, your CPA, and your wealth advisor. Beyond the obvious ways to vet them, be sure you do the chemistry check. Will you look forward to talking to them down the road? Here are a couple of questions we find revealing when asked of any professional:

- What is your favorite type of client situation to work with?
- How do you stay current in your profession?
- How does my situation compare with your other clients?
- Who backs you up if you are away when I need you?

Again, these are probably similar questions to those you've used to hire business consultants over the years. They will serve you just as well when it comes to building your own Wealth Regeneration team.

In the chapters ahead we will often refer to your advisor. In most cases, this will be your wealth advisor. To be most valuable that individual will need multiple skill sets, in planning, forecasting, and investing, to name a few. In Appendix 1 we have included a more detailed checklist for selecting a wealth advisor. Still, your ability and instincts about choosing great teammates that has served you so well over the years should carry the day. Pay attention to them.

Holding People Accountable

This is one rule that almost goes without saying. It's unlikely you'd be where you are today if you had not embraced accountability both personally and as the art of holding others accountable. The elements are:

- Defining goals.
- Setting the targets and benchmarks.
- Conducting a periodic review.
- Accepting consequences.

In the venue of your personal life a businesslike approach to accountability can require some thought and patience to pull off. We find that many leaders, while very willing to hold business colleagues accountable, may get quite squeamish when it comes to accountability for themselves, their family members, or personal friends.

This is in many ways the least complex of the business skills we want you to bring to your own transition planning. Yet it may take the most willpower to put in place. So let's say you hire a personal trainer to assist you in getting healthier. Feeling good and staying healthy over your lifetime are often major transition goals. You want to feel good for as long as you possibly can. Who wouldn't? Yet you find you're always canceling those appointments. Something "more important" always comes up. There's that pesky accountability thing lurking again.

And don't even get us started on how hard it is to apply these principles to your kids! Never fear, we have some ideas that you may find useful later on. But those ideas will lack viability if you fail to practice accountability on yourself.

Meaningful Work

How have you inspired others in the past? What got them fired up and moving forward? You know, and research supports, that it is not just about economic rewards. It's about meaningful work.

One of the most bankrupt premises of traditional retirement planning is that your goal is to "work so you don't have to." We say balderdash to that! It seems to us that this demeans what you have spent a lifetime doing, rather than seeing your work as a stepping-stone to what's next.

Over your career you have marshaled your skills and intellect to create value. You have found it amazingly fulfilling. Why wouldn't you want to keep doing this in some form or fashion? If you discover that you can afford not to be paid, so much the better. You just have more choices.

This is not to suggest that you stay in the same career or business. Far from it. Only that the productive habits of a lifetime are not so easily overthrown. There is a joy in productivity. You'll want to keep that throughout your lifetime. Why wouldn't you?

You've Got This Wired

So you see, nothing you need to do to put disciplined lifelong strategy into place is new to you. You have this totally wired. These are skills that already come naturally to you. We will just be asking you to tap these existing skills in new ways. At last, you'll be addressing your own life as the very important business proposition that it is.

PARTING THOUGHTS

1. What do you believe it takes to plan well?
2. Do you have a reputation as a leader with a specific approach? What is it?
3. What's the first thing you do when you tackle a big project?

CHAPTER 5

Leading in a New Way

You know, getting old isn't all that bad. We have been pussyfooting around so far when it comes to talking about aging—"the inevitable effects of aging" and all that—but there are some effects of aging that are clear-cut bonuses:

- Less concern about what others may think (one of Kaycee's personal favorites).
- A measure of equanimity. Now when you say "nobody died" you know what it actually means.
- A new respect for the passage of time. Before you might have been time driven, but now you want to savor it.
- An even lower tolerance for fools. Do we even need to elaborate on this?

All to the good, and in some ways fair compensation for achy knees.

What Is Generativity?

Perhaps the most powerful positive impact is the urge toward a thing called generativity. Eric Erickson, renowned psychologist and Harvard professor (perhaps best known for coining the phrase "identity crisis"), first described it. Erickson saw generativity as that stage in life when you begin to care more about others and their future than your own. With generativity, you begin to see success differently, not so much as what you have accomplished as what others have accomplished.

In the context of what we've been talking about—what's next in your life—this may be the biggest factor yet.

Many people tell us they experience generativity as an itch or a yearning to make things better for those who will come after them. Erickson put it in procreative terms (he was a student of Anna Freud so perhaps he couldn't help it), but it is so much more than just biology. In fact, discovering how you might be generative and becoming generative on your own terms is quite possibly the key to embracing all of life's transitions.

We define generativity as the impulse to give back, make things better, and work to see others succeed. What kinds of things are generative? Clearly, generativity is in the eye of the beholder. For most of us it is experienced in multiple ways; for example:

- Quality time with a child.
- Mentoring a young adult.
- Volunteering for causes we care about.

And it may retain a connection to one's career even after retirement:

- Providing leadership in one's professional association.
- Creating new intellectual property.
- Enabling others to succeed as we have succeeded.

It can also take the shape of a brand-new activity, something you've never done before:

- Learning a new art form and then doing a lot of it, maybe even selling it.
- Starting a brand-new business.
- Becoming a fund-raiser for charity.

Obviously the list can be very long. You may find multiple ways to be generative that are appealing. You may even pursue all of them simultaneously. The choice is yours.

Generativity Is Leadership

Generativity is a form of leadership, perhaps one of the highest forms. If you believe (as we do) that the heart of being a leader is inspiring, supporting, enabling, and nourishing others to move forward, you'll see how generativity is the natural extension of leadership. Whether it's with professional colleagues or family members, those in need in your community or dear friends, whenever you are working to inspire, support, enable, and nourish, you are practicing generativity. At its peak generative leadership seeks positive outcomes for others that they are able to manage and continue on their own. When they don't need you any more, you have succeeded. That's truly generative.

Think about generativity in terms of direct human interaction. The reality is, it happens in many modalities. Artists and writers are practicing generativity when they send their work off into the world for others to experience. Teachers are by definition generative. Any activity that inspires, supports, enables, and nourishes is generative. And there is no doubt that generativity and leadership are two faces of the same impulse.

In many cultures this kind of activity is seen as the proper work of those called elders. Whether you want to call yourself an elder or not, whenever you deploy your life experience and skills to move others along their way, generativity is deeply embedded in it.

Jay Hughes, one of the world's foremost experts on families and wealth, has written extensively on eldering. In an essay entitled *A Reflection on the Traits and Capacities of Family Elders*[1] he describes an elder's demeanor and actions as she leads others forward in a generative manner: "An elder carries within herself the ability to discover where the larger truth lies . . . not simply what the facts suggest. She can do this because part of her life journey has been learning to discover and define. She uses this process to help others find theirs." Clearly this is leadership at its most generative.

Have It Your Way

For us work intensives, embracing generativity does come with some twists. Can we be satisfied with having our generativity piecemeal? This is actually the most common pattern during retirement and highly satisfying for many people. Case in point: perhaps you decide to volunteer as a counselor to small business owners. Do you want to be in a position where you are just available to people at certain times a few days a week? Do you see this as more of a second career, although less stressful? Or do you need more intensity in your generativity? Do you prefer a nonprofit startup? At some point do you need a step-down approach? Note that there is no right or wrong answer here—the key is figuring out what is right for you.

One comment we hear frequently is "I am busier now than when I was working." We sometimes hear it paired with "and I'm not sure exactly what

---

[1] This essay is available on Jay's website at: www.jamesehughes.com

I'm doing all day long." We see this as an indicator that some conscious thought about being generative is in order.

It's About Regeneration

We have called what we are asking you to do here—Wealth Regeneration—for a reason. Generativity is at the core of it. You can't have regeneration unless you have something to regenerate with, whether it's your time, your treasure, or your talents. All are aspects of your wealth. As you look at your own real life in the exercises ahead, we believe you'll see much to build upon. It is likely you've already been generative as the foundation of your success. You are already in the midst of generativity; you just didn't have a name for yet. You've been leading all your life, so for you, generativity is just leading in a new way. And Wealth Regeneration positions you to be strategic about it.

PARTING THOUGHTS

1. Can you name an example of generativity in someone you admire?
2. What kinds of things are you already doing that are generative?
3. Are there things you wish you were doing that seem generative, but you just aren't getting around to them? What are they?

PART II

The Wealth Regeneration Discipline

CHAPTER 6

The Concept of the Wheel

Simply put, a wheel is a circle, and the Wealth Regeneration Wheel is just that. Our wheel is based upon a classic process circle, the foundation of human endeavor since we were all in caves. The Wheel looks like every process diagram you've ever seen in business. Yet there are key differences. It's about you, not a business. And it's designed to roll forward, that's why we call it a wheel.

To go back to all of us living in caves for a moment, the classic process wheel is simply four steps:

1. Figure out where you are (I'm at home in my comfy cave, but I am hungry).
2. Figure out what you want (I'd like to bring home some tasty mastodon meat for dinner).
3. Figure out how to get it done (a bunch of us will grab our spears and go hunting).
4. Then do it.

It begins simply as a line . . .

Hungry   Well-Fed

. . . but because human life has multiple needs and goals—many ongoing and often simultaneous—it becomes a circle, and in the best of circumstances ultimately becomes a wheel. Figure 6.1 shows how.

FIGURE 6.1   It's a Circle

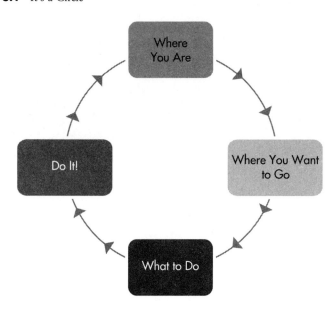

Circle to Wheel

In real life, again from our cave person's perspective, our subject wakes up the next day to say "Oh, I'm hungry again." That's how it works. And the logical thing is for the circle to go around one more time. There is no need to step beyond the circle. Won't mastodon meat be our preferred cuisine forever?

So how does it become a wheel? What makes things change? A will toward progress, a desire for more, and what was linear becomes circular and what is circular now rolls forward. You might think this is obvious—it is and it isn't. Throughout history entire civilizations became extinct when they became too entrenched in their circle and unable to follow it forward into a wheel. They could not see that they were stuck in the rut. Things were working, so why change? Yet the wheel is the agent for all significant human progress, sometimes quite unwittingly. The question becomes how to make turning the wheel natural and intentional.

Does our subject decide to go beyond hunting? So maybe it now goes like this:

- Figure out where you are (here I am in my comfy cave, hungry but too tired to hunt).
- Figure out what you want (something to eat).
- Figure out how to get there (send the women out to find nuts and berries).
- Then do it.

As you can see, these are simply iterations. So what's next? Farming, as seen in Figure 6.2!

FIGURE 6.2 Farming

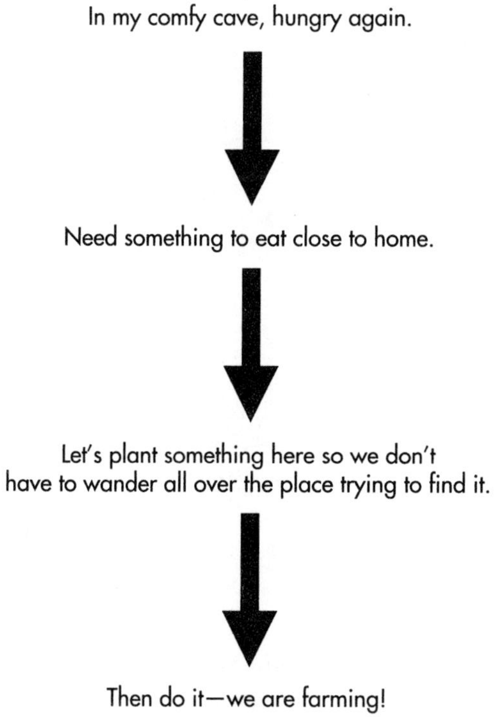

In my comfy cave, hungry again.

Need something to eat close to home.

Let's plant something here so we don't
have to wander all over the place trying to find it.

Then do it—we are farming!

The circle truly becomes a wheel when it moves you forward as shown in Figure 6.3. Now you may be thinking—so what? Isn't this obvious? Isn't this what you do in life and business every day? Well, it may be obvious, but we can tell you it is rarely practiced with thought or intent, particularly in personal life.

FIGURE 6.3 The Circle Becomes a Wheel

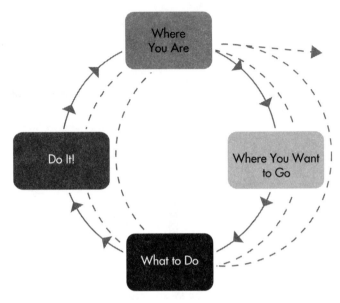

Successful and innovative businesses make turning the wheel as natural as breathing and that's what moves them forward. But they would be hard pressed to explain it to you. Those that fail to turn the wheel may not even survive. And they may not even realize why, until the facts turn up in a business school case study. It is also no surprise that the eager MBA student who leaps on those facts would probably fail to recognize the same pattern in his or her own life. Can you be smarter than that?

Dealing with Change

The wheel—particularly when it bumps you forward—is the most fundamental way humans deal with change. As you have experienced, both personally and as a leader, change management is one of the biggest challenges you face. There are shelves of books written on the subject, and with good reason. Change is hard.

Human nature is to stay in the circle—just keep hunting the mastodon—not roll forward like a wheel to new foods and new ways of obtaining them.

Whoever said the definition of crazy is continuing to do the same thing over and over again and expecting a different result had it nailed. That is the classic description of being stuck in the circle.

The challenge is to create momentum. Not by abandoning the circle process (which has worked for millennia) but by managing it on purpose in such a way that it becomes a wheel and so moves you forward. Throughout your career, you undoubtedly have done this again and again. You carefully nudged people from their comfortable circle to the forward motion represented by the wheel. And sometimes it took more than a nudge!

What's Next?

Now as you consider what's next for your own life the same equations apply. Traditional planning for retirement is very linear. It says "Let's figure out how much money is needed, then you can go to:

A. The desert,
B. Florida, or
C. Another sunny place,

And:

A. Play golf forever,
B. Play tennis forever,
C. Write your memoirs."

Please! This fails on a number of levels, not the least of which is because it is soul-numbingly simplistic. Your life is too complicated to be placed in such a narrow box. No wonder so many baby boomers are avoiding thinking about it altogether.

Here's the reality: We live in times when change is rampant. You will change, the economy will change, and the world will change. Only a very thoughtful and intentional mastery of the wheel is likely to get you through whatever comes your way in the second half of life. A mere circle will not cut it.

And by the way, we are not against living in warm places or golf/tennis/ memoirs. What we are against is arranging your life on the assumption that any one circle is likely to be sustainable over the rest of your life. Anything could happen, and it will.

You Know How to Do This

As someone who has experience as a leader you are ahead of most people when it comes to the wheel. You have had hands-on experience moving lines to circles and circles to wheels or you wouldn't be in the position you are in today. You get how essential this is on an almost molecular level.

Interestingly, you may find that you have trouble applying this to yourself. Most people do. You are fantastic at dealing with the essential nature of the wheel in your business life but you go all linear, or maybe circular, when it comes to dealing with your own affairs. This is made more difficult by the financial services industry and the media. The information you get, even from the best resources, is usually either linear or at best circular. After all, they want you to make a decision and stay put! It will be up to you to convert it to the wheel. And we're here to help you cut through it all.

Our goal in the following chapters is to help you mobilize the skills you already have to apply them on your own behalf. In this way you can create a consistent discipline for forward motion, in short, your very own wheel.

As you think about your own road ahead you know that changes are inevitable. Some you will choose, some will be thrust upon you. Treating life as linear is clearly flawed, and expecting only one circle to be sustainable throughout the remainder of your lifetime is unrealistic.

That's why the intentional and consistent use of the wheel is so essential. It is the thing that gets you through change no matter what gets thrown in your way.

To be brutally honest, and to avoid coming off like a couple of Pollyannas, we must admit that in life the wheel does not always roll forward. Tragically, things like drug addiction, mental illness, or sheer bad luck can cause slippage. Yet that reality does not diminish its power. The value of understanding and acknowledging the power of the wheel as an agent of human progress lies in your ability to harness it. It's your wheel to use as you see fit.

Get It Rolling

So how do you get your personal wheel going? We suspect you may already have a number of the key elements in play; you just haven't thought about it in a disciplined strategic way. In the next section we lay out a road map for you to do just that.

Back to our cavemen for a moment. The pace of change they faced was quite literally glacial. Their original circles—"let's hunt"—took millennia to evolve to the next level, "let's farm." None of us have that luxury today. The arrays of things already flying at us that require us to adapt are daunting.

Many are things we can't even envision right now. We certainly never expected in our lifetimes to need to learn how to "tweet," let alone text.

We are willing to bet that in your career, you have done everything you can to make your organization adaptable and nimble. And you've done it for your family as well. That means, whether you thought about it that way or not, making the kind of strategic thinking embedded in the wheel a part of everyday life is as natural to you as breathing. You've been the one to ask others, "What else can we do here?" All we are suggesting is that you do the same for your own self, in your own life.

A Kick in the . . .

In typical situations, human nature is very prone to staying with the status quo. That means forward motion from the circle to the wheel tends to occur only when the familiar becomes uncomfortable for some reason. Perhaps something big (and possibly bad) happens. Or things just aren't working as they used to. These things conspire to create a sense of urgency, and then things move. Maybe it's because mastodons became hard to find that farming arose, or maybe competition from other humans made farming more attractive. Or maybe all the kids decided to become vegans (kidding).

In business, it often takes an economic downturn before real change is made. Or maybe it is an unfriendly merger or a failed product line. These are the commercial versions of something big and possibly bad that can and does happen. When it comes to your own life, it's likely this is just as true. A trigger to move forward can be a health crisis, the sale of the business, or the loss of a job. These are all great reasons to be looking at what's next.

Yet it is even more powerful to be looking ahead to what's next just for the sake of looking ahead. In business that is how you stay ahead of the competition, so think about how that might work in your personal life. Make a practice of looking over the horizon and considering what's next even when everything seems to be fine, because you never know what you might see. We find it is rarely a bad idea to be ahead of the game.

But whatever gets you going, once you are ready for a change, we urge you to go beyond merely creating a new circle for yourself. Why? Because we can guarantee you that any single circle is unlikely to have lasting value. Something will happen to make it no longer fit, and you'll be right back in today's pickle figuring out what's next. So you might as well create a wheel for yourself from the get-go.

Looking at What Happens

In our view the linchpin of moving any circle into a wheel is feedback, data, accountability, or whatever you prefer to call it (see Figure 6.4). A habit of honestly assessing what happened and why it happened is essential. When you're within a circle the data that support staying in that circle are often the easiest to see. Your job is to filter through them and find the data that are most relevant to who you are and where you are going. What happened? What's next? Answering these questions is the only way you can determine whether or not your current actions are good enough or additional action needs to be taken.

If you agree that the impetus for change is discomfort, you won't be surprised to find that asking the tough questions can provide just the push needed. Sometimes knowing "what happened" and "what's next" is all that is needed to roll the wheel forward.

Of course, this is not simply about change for change's sake. If after taking the hard look you find your current circle is serving you well, good news. You may choose to run things around that same circle multiple times, maybe even for years. The point is being able to identify when something *else*

FIGURE 6.4   Rolling the Wheel Forward

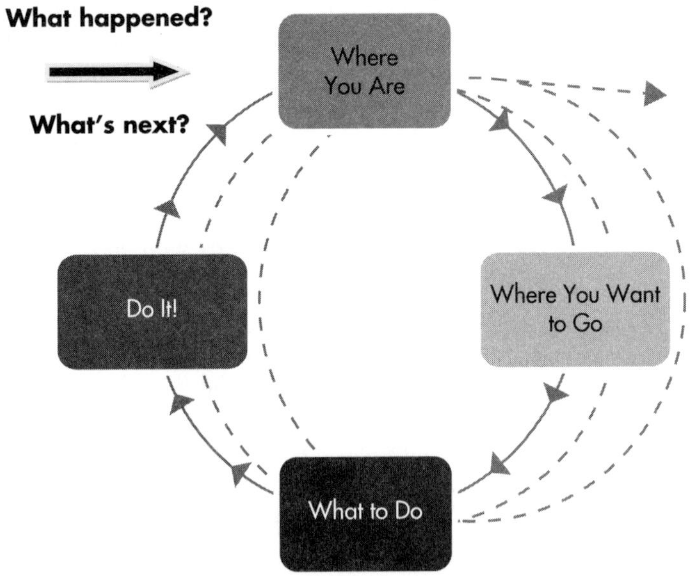

is needed sooner rather than later. That is what makes asking what happened and what's next so valuable—so that you can get to any change while you have the most opportunity to maintain your forward momentum.

We urge you to incorporate the concept of the wheel into your repertoire now. Don't wait for your current circle to become outmoded. The reality is that circles retraced over time tend to become very tactical. The challenge in maintaining the wheel is to pull yourself up to some more strategic viewpoint. When it's about "let's get some mastodon meat," it's tactical. When it becomes "let's have plenty to eat in the safety of our comfy cave," it becomes strategic. Like it or not, you'll need to create your own vision for the future. That's what gets the wheel rolling, and that's what pulls this entire process up into the realm of strategy.

Thinking this way when it comes to your personal life is not always the most comfortable approach. In real life we may want to let the sleeping dogs sleep on. But we have found the very act of rigorously going through the process not only increases long-term success for our clients but provides amazing peace of mind as well. At this point in your life, you not only want success, you'd also like to sleep at night. The discipline of the wheel can give you both.

PROFILE: TOM CAMPION

Tom Campion is the former CEO and currently chairman of the board of the company he cofounded in 1978, Zumiez. Today Zumiez, a publicly traded company, is considered to be the largest action sports lifestyle retailer in the world. And if we had to pick a word to describe Tom Campion, it would certainly be action.

Tom styles himself as "just a salesman," having spent his entire career in retail. He began in the grocery business, then on to JCPenney as a management trainee before founding his own stores. Like many in the 1960s he worked his way through school, graduated from college with a degree in political science, and then had to go out and find himself a job in the real world.

The key to Tom's great success is his ability to inspire others to action. He is especially proud of the sales culture at Zumiez, one that has produced year-over-year increases in same-store sales for 29 out of the first 30 years. When he talks about his "sales kids," as he calls them, he uses the word *embolden*—and it is inspiring or perhaps inciting boldness that is the center of Tom's life today.

(continued)

In 1961, as a teenager, Tom went on his first backpacking trip with a youth group. Being in the wilderness for that initial time was an epiphany for him. There began a lifetime love of wide open spaces. Throughout his career, even as he juggled business and family, he always made time for the outdoors. This included active efforts to save old-growth habitats and a chance to start using that political science degree. Tom actually knows how to call in a spotted owl and stop a logging truck!

In 1980, Tom made his first trip to Alaska and immediately recognized that Alaska—in particular the Arctic—represented one of the last great wilderness places in the world. He thought it needed to be preserved for future generations. In his usual fashion, Tom set about protecting this amazing place using the most formidable of his skills—salesmanship.

Throughout his career Tom has understood how to get the attention of customers in ways that closed the deal. While at JCPenney he managed virtually every department in the store, from the customer complaints department to ladies' foundations, all with extraordinary results. A signature moment occurred when he was managing housewares. There, in order to move a batch of Weber barbecues, he fired up one of the barbecues in the middle of the store, had a ham thrown on it, let the smell waft out through the mall, and immediately got customers' attention. Needless to say, barbecues flew out the door.

Tom knew that to inspire the zeal necessary to protect the wild areas of Alaska, people had to actually *see* the place. He needed to connect the customer to the product, just like firing up that barbecue. He was about to do the same thing for Alaska.

As an advocate for the Alaska Wilderness League, Tom began to organize expeditions for those in a position to affect the future of the Arctic: senators, members of Congress, and others in the seats of power. His invitations were accepted. In the first few years his intrepid co-adventurers included Dick Durbin and Maria Cantwell.

Over the last 10 years there have been three attempts in Congress to begin drilling in the Arctic. These have been thwarted at least in part thanks to the army of believers that Tom has created by bringing people face to face with the Arctic and its beauty—in a sense, lighting the barbecue so they could see how it worked and why they needed one.

Today Tom's passion for the Arctic wilderness continues unabated. While still remaining an icon within Zumiez, he has transferred day-to-day leadership to a leadership team. Now, he has started his own family foundation. His goal is to keep making a difference day after day. He is working just as hard as he always has, doing what comes naturally, selling. Only now instead of skateboards and sneakers, his product is a vision of a wilderness always free for future generations to enjoy. That vision can be seen most dramatically in *To the Arctic*, an IMAX movie that Tom recently co-produced. You can check out the trailer at www.welcometothearctic.org.

When asked about the future, Tom puts it best. He says, "Some guys want big headstones with blinky, blinky lights. That's not me. I want things to happen right now." And that's just how he rolls.

How are you going to roll?

CHAPTER 7

Know Where You Are

The best place to start any journey is almost always at the beginning. That means knowing where you are and—to the extent possible—*why* you are where you are. It is just common sense that there is no forward motion without knowing and understanding your starting position. If sometimes that means you must rehash ancient history, so be it. That's what you would tell anyone on your team, so that's where you begin when it comes to yourself. Where are you today?

We propose that you assess three key elements to obtain the most clear-eyed view of your present situation:

1. **Defining Your Wealth**—When you say the word *wealth*, what does that mean to you? Your real wealth goes beyond the traditional definitions of assets and liabilities. It is up to you to define it. What matters most to you? How do you measure all aspects of your wealth, both your human capital and your financial capital? We will suggest you implement a dual balance sheet approach.

2. **Lifestyle Analysis**—Does your lifestyle support or hinder your goals? When was the last time you took a detailed look at it? At various points in this process you'll be considering how your existing assets stack up against what you need. Most research suggests that we all do a woefully inadequate job of costing out our lifestyle. Do you really know what your cost of living is today? You need to know this.

3. **Personal History Review**—Who are you and where did you come from? This is not about writing your memoirs, nor is it therapy. It's about looking back at your life for clues as to what might make the most satisfying "what's next" as well as what truly matters most to you.

We will cover how to define your wealth and analyze your lifestyle in this chapter. We will also cover how to determine if your wealth is sustainable over your lifetime. Reviewing personal history is a separate art form, so we will devote another chapter to that.

Now if you haven't already done so, this is the perfect time to engage your advisor in the process. We will provide examples here of tools you can use, but you may find your advisor has other equally valid ways of attacking the project. We suggest you use their tools whenever possible. And if you have questions about finding a good advisor, see Appendix 1.

Defining Your Wealth

We have agreed that your real wealth includes more than just your financial wherewithal. Your human capital with its wealth of relationships, knowledge, and values must be addressed as well.

The Dual Balance Sheet

The place to begin in understanding your real wealth is with the time-tested balance sheet. Even when talking about human capital, you might ask? Yes indeed, we reply. The beauty of an old-fashioned balance sheet is that it draws the complex elements of any situation together in a way that looks at a specific point in time and measures both positives and negatives. Just what the doctor ordered.

If you think of a financial balance sheet in its simplest terms, it is this: what you own minus what you owe equals what you've got. That's the real definition of net worth. Done right, it is a freeze-frame—a snapshot—of a particular moment. Prepared in a consistent fashion over time, it provides the best track record. You can truly test whether progress has been made if you place balance sheets from two different time periods side-by-side. It's always enlightening.

As you turn to your human capital, the same balance sheet principles apply. Although calling it a balance sheet when it is prepared on the human side is unusual, it still makes preeminently good sense. It is simply a consistent and more measurable way of doing what Kaycee's mom always called "counting your blessings and making your list." (Betty was a great believer that you could accomplish anything in life as long as you had a good list.) Again, the goal is to create snapshots of moments in time that can be used to determine if forward progress has been made and assess the quality of that progress.

Financial Capital

We'd be surprised if you didn't already have a way of looking at your financial net worth. Most successful people do. Although we would also be surprised if you had looked at it any time recently. When was the last time you looked at your net worth? Maybe the last time you borrowed money? It's time to take a look at it again. Whatever format you already have in place is probably just fine. And again, your accountant or advisor may already have this going for you, so grab whatever you can. What is critical here is how you use it. A simplified example of what we're talking about is in Figure 7.1.

Ask yourself these questions:

• *How often do I actually pull it together and look at it?* It's sad but true that busy and successful people often just don't pay attention. That may have worked okay when things were going well (ignorance can be bliss), but when change is on the horizon, it's a risk. At least once a year is a must.
• *How honest am I about what's in it?* The enemy of financial security is overly optimistic assumptions. When it comes to listing the value of your assets, whether it's your home or your business, realism is a must. Be cautious about how you list inheritances and trusts. Unless and until you own them outright, they are not technically your assets.
• *Did I acknowledge the differences in liquidity?* As you know, the measure of liquidity in any asset is how quickly it can flow back into spendable money. It's always smart to arrange things in order of liquidity—cash first and then on down the line. Just as you would in a business setting.

FIGURE 7.1 Balance Sheet for Financial Capital

	Assets	Liabilities
Liquid Assets		
Retirement Assets		
Other Assets		
Personal Assets		
TOTALS		

ASSETS   –   LIABILITIES   =   NET WORTH

The points so far are fairly clear-cut. Here are a few areas where things get more nuanced:

- *What about hidden taxes?* Everyone has assets that can create tax liability when they are used or sold. Many of us look at retirement assets at their full value, yet because of how IRAs and pensions are taxed when you take them out, that value can be misleading.
- *What about hidden liabilities?* Have you been generous with family members by offering to guarantee or cosign debts or leases? Have you personally guaranteed business debt? In these times such liabilities can become very real.
- *Have you listed all liabilities? Are they noted as to when they come due and what their terms are?* A trap more than a few successful people have fallen into in recent years is borrowing over relatively short periods of time on the assumption that things can always be refinanced. Well, as you know, *all* assumptions now need to be checked at the door.

You'll note in our example that we like to see assets and liabilities listed side-by-side in order of liquidity. We think this makes it easier to assess how they might interact.

For slippery points like the ones above we suggest the habit of foot-noting. Now, we expect your advisor will undoubtedly be plugging hidden taxes or ballooning debts into proper spreadsheets. But you need to keep track of these things as well. Straightforward notes on the face of the statement are an easy and convenient way to do this. Then, every time you pull it out for review, you are reminded of what's there and what is not. And a footnote is a perfect place to mention what Aunt Millie may have left for you inside her teapot.

Just a comment about frequency. As you look at putting together a Wealth Regeneration plan for what's next for yourself and for your family, there will be a number of points where numeric measurements are essential. With the combination of ready technology and economic volatility, it is tempting to want to take these measurements too often. **Don't** succumb to the temptation. Used properly these are tools to monitor and impact *long-term* trends in your personal wealth. Overused, they become a distraction and can suck you into very short-term thinking, to your peril. Remember, just because technology makes some things easy, it doesn't make them a good idea. The right frequency varies with the nature of the analysis. We'll talk about that more as we progress.

At the end of this chapter we provide for you an example of a more detailed financial balance sheet. Feel free to tweak it in whatever way works best for you, or substitute another format. The goal is just getting it done.

Human Capital

This is where the rubber truly meets the road. While you have probably prepared a financial balance sheet at least once in your life (you bought a house, didn't you?), you may never have prepared such a thing for your human capital. Yet when we ask our clients critical questions like "What do you truly value?" or "What gets you up in the morning?" the answers are always in the human capital realm. It is never about the money, although it may be about what the money can do.

All we are suggesting is that you bring a level of intentionality and focus to tending your human capital just as you would on the financial side.

When it comes to human capital, there is no one way to define assets and liabilities. When it comes to measuring human capital over time, the field is totally wide open. We recognize that lifetimes of work and volumes of literature have gone into understanding the meaning of human capital. So let us apologize in advance for the simplicity of this tool. It does get the job done, however.

What we seek to do here is to lay out the essential elements of human capital in a way that enables you to engage in fairly straightforward assessment and measurement of human capital as you define it over time. Wasn't it Drucker who said "What gets measured gets managed"? That's what we're talking about. The reality is that this will be very personal and highly subjective. It is about you, after all, so it needs to be in terms that are meaningful for you and potentially for your loved ones as well. What we think at the end of the day won't matter.

Here's how it works. On one sheet of paper (or a spreadsheet) we lay out the four categories that we find most people want to measure as part of their human capital. They are:

Well-being
Relationships
Fulfillment
Legacy

You can think of these as the asset classes of your life. You may want to add or delete from this list; that's just fine. This is about your human capital,

FIGURE 7.2   Aspects of Human Capital

Well-Being

- Health
- Peace of mind
- Lifestyle
- Learning and growth

Relationships

- Spouse or partner
- Immediate family
- Extended family
- Friends
- Business colleagues

Fulfillment

- Work
- Creativity
- Community
- Philanthropy
- Politics

Legacy

- Immediate family
- Extended family
- Friends
- Community
- Profession/business
- Politics

after all. Within each category are more specific aspects. You can see what we suggest in Figure 7.2. Health is under well-being, for example. You can tailor this to suit. Just make sure it includes all the things that matter most to you.

Not all the items on the list may apply in your particular case, so add or delete at will! Truly, feel free to make this entirely your own. For Kaycee her dogs fit under the well-being category; for Bob, let's just say it's not dogs.

You'll note we have left out spirituality. It's not that we don't think it's important—we do, as do many of our clients. But we find each person has very specific ideas about where spirituality fits for them. Is it a part of well-being? Is it its own category? Or is it just so much a part of everything there is no need to call it out? You make the call.

You might also be thinking about the difference between fulfillment and legacy. As we use it here, fulfillment is about those things you do in your life today, paid or unpaid, to add meaning and give you satisfaction. As a leader, we hope your career has met the definition of fulfilling. What other activities provide meaning and satisfaction to you? Legacy covers those contributions that you hope survive you. We will devote one of our final chapters to how you recognize and build your personal legacy.

When asked what we really do (and in the company of those with a sense of humor), we respond like this, "It is our job to make sure that our clients have all the resources they need for their lifetimes and the peace of mind to enjoy them. And that when they are gone, at least as many people have good reason to celebrate their life, as seek an inheritance." Isn't that what it's really all about? Having your life matter at the end of the day, not just your money? Assessing human capital is essential if you want to fully complete this task.

Some are surprised that a wealth manager focuses so much on this. Yet when it comes to personal wealth, as opposed to endowments or corporate pension plans, say, enhancement of human capital ultimately becomes the point of the exercise. Why have the financial resources at your disposal at all if they don't make life better for yourself, your loved ones, and the causes you care about?

As a result, we believe that the goals and dreams for the human side should absolutely drive the financial side. When financial decisions are made about risk, liquidity, diversification, and complexity, they can and should reflect what the human values and hopes to achieve. Our clients—whether old money or new—see their wealth as a launching pad, not an end in itself. The Wealth Regeneration discipline was created with that in mind. Hence the desire to measure "performance" on the human side, just as it is measured on the investment side.

So once you have laid out all the aspects in a way that makes sense to you, you can move to making the assessments. We use an approach that is almost embarrassingly straightforward—pluses and minuses. No need to be overly analytic about this; a simple thumbs up or thumbs down will do. Figure 7.3 gives you an example of how someone might fill out one of the categories, that of well-being.

Particularly note the comments section. Comments are incredibly important here. They provide a sense of the context in which you are assigning a plus or minus score. Comments also often guide next actions. As you see in this example, there is a deficit on the learning and growth side. An action has been noted, "sign up for cooking school in France." This kind of comment can be used in the future to determine whether progress has been made at the next human capital review.

This exercise is particularly valuable when a couple fills it out separately, then compares notes. You can also see that reflected in the comments in

FIGURE 7.3   Example of Human Capital Assessment

Well-Being	Assets	Liabilities	Comments
• Health	++		
• Peace of mind	+	–	One of us worries no matter what ☺.
• Lifestyle	++		
• Learning/Growth		–	We need to get out more—sign up for cooking school in France, or . . . ?
TOTALS	5	2	

Figure 7.3. It can often help set family priorities when time or resource constraints are at issue.

Not all of our clients prepare a human capital balance sheet in exactly this way. And some that choose to do so still keep the scores private. However, all do provide us with the information about their human capital priorities with enough focus to make key decisions with those priorities in mind. And those priorities are tracked over time. If you are not now sharing this kind of data with your key advisers, we suggest that you do. We have no doubt that better outcomes, both personal and financial, will result.

Lifestyle Analysis—How Much Is Enough?

Looking at your human capital is also the best vantage point for a discussion of spending. As you look at your lifestyle from this perspective, some items may pop out that don't make sense—or you may confirm that it's just right, you love how you are living your life. At this point in the process it's not necessary to make any judgments about your lifestyle. You just need to understand what it is and how much it really costs. These are essential ingredients in determining what it takes to keep your lifestyle and your goals sustainable.

Perhaps you have kept records of spending. That always makes the job of analyzing lifestyle costs much easier. Or maybe you haven't. In either case, going back through or looking at the last two to five years of your spending is worth the effort. It needs to be done, even if you have to hire someone to help you do it. Here are some of the kinds of things that a thoughtful look at your past history may help decode:

- *Have your children really left home?* Even though they're through with school, you might be surprised at the level of support you are providing that slips under the radar. Somehow, you fail to recognize that paying their car insurance premium and perhaps buying their groceries can be as much of a drain in its way as college tuition. How long do you expect to go on? And how much is it, really?
- *Do you have more than one home?* It's important to tease out the real cost of each home. Often you may just see that your annual nut when it comes to property taxes is a big number. Do you plan to keep all the homes? When you see the individual expense, does your actual use justify it?
- *Does your business pick up expenses that you would pay personally if you were not working?* For many successful executives and business owners the expense of cell phones, cars, and perhaps travel (as examples) are at least partially or completely paid by their organization. Taking over these expenses personally can come as a rude surprise at the point of transition. You'll want to be aware this.
- *What kind of charitable contributions do you make?* Are there some things you do because it's expected in your role? Will you stop making those contributions if your role changes? Are there other gifts you would like to make?

Now you may be thinking that we are suggesting that you do a budget. Well, kind of but not really. A real budget is forward-looking. Right now it's essential that you look back and identify if there are any major areas that might change. Definitely do not assume that your cost of living will go down dramatically if you transition to something else at this point in your life. For most people (as in many things in life) past history may be your best predictor of the future.

At the end of this chapter we lay out an example of the types of spending categories that you may want to consider on Worksheet 3. If you are already keeping detailed financial records and are using different kinds of categories, don't worry about it. However, if you haven't been, this list of categories can help guide you in pulling together the data in the most meaningful way to be used as a look forward.

And in reality, once you get to the analytics, too much detailed categorization gets in the way. This is about the big picture. And in the big picture, only major categories are needed. In fact, we are able to do analysis for clients even if they only bring us one number: "Here is what I need every year." The trick is making sure that that one number really covers everything. It must be realistic.

How Sustainable Is Your Wealth?

The sustainability of wealth varies greatly from person to person. It is not merely a number; it is an amalgamation of all the factors that make up your situation. At its core must be some very rigorous and forward-looking financial analysis. In business terms this analysis is like an asset and liability matching study done over your lifetime. It has actuarial elements. Properly done, it is overlaid with economic risk assessment. Think of this as a very long range personal financial forecast. (See Appendix 2 for a discussion of how to determine if this is being correctly done for you.)

As in any analysis that purports to see the future, the view is inherently imperfect. Yet we see these analyses as essential in two ways. First, they provide you with a realistic and disciplined way to see what's possible. Additionally, performed with a consistent methodology over regular intervals, they provide guidance for course correction.

At this point, you want to start with a baseline analysis of the sustainability of your wealth. It includes what you know today and basic assumptions about future spending. Its goal is to set the stage for more complex analysis over time.

Understanding what's possible can be eye opening. We use a device called the Wealth Continuum to help clients visualize it. While the realm of possibilities under consideration clearly has a financial basis, the answer is essentially a human equation. Take a look at Figure 7.4. Do you know where you fit today? Do you know where you'd like to fit? That is what sustainability analysis is all about.

One of our favorite analogies is that of the jumbo jet flying from Honolulu to Los Angeles. Any seasoned pilot will tell you that the plane is always slightly off course. In the old days it was the pilot's job (now it's the autopilot) to tweak things on an ongoing basis to stay on course. You want

FIGURE 7.4   The Wealth Continuum

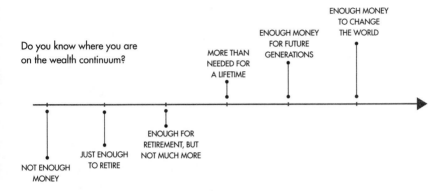

to stay on course too. This kind of sustainability analysis is what helps you do that. And real life often requires much more tweaking than a plane flight.

Once your baseline sustainability is in place, you will be able to assess more clearly what your transition choices might mean. Are you considering moving? A new career as a teacher? A large charitable contribution? You're now positioned to make truly informed decisions.

Well, clearly you have had your work cut out for you just to get this far. Let us remind you again that your advisors may already have much of this pulled together for you. Don't hesitate to leverage what they know. Because next we get to the fun part—talking about you and where you want to go from here.

PROFILE: DICK PECHTER

By anyone's standards, Dick Pechter fit the Wall Street stereotype of a "master of the universe." The CEO of Donaldson Lufkin Jenrette Financial Services (DLJ) and the chairman of DLJ Direct, up until his retirement in early 2000, Dick had begun his career at DLJ in 1969, when there were only about 90 employees. At his retirement there were 16,000 employees.

Dick spent his career at DLJ building and growing internal business units. He jokes, "I did whatever anybody else didn't want to do." And he

(continued)

was clearly very good at it. Several of these businesses became enormously successful in their own right, including Pershing and DLJ Direct, which went on to become a part of E*TRADE.

Dick is one of those folks that self-deprecatingly attributes his success to luck and happenstance. But it is clearly so much more than that. Laced throughout his stories of happy accidents is a clear pattern of the willingness to say "why not?"—and take the consequences if something failed.

DLJ Direct is a great example of this. In the mid-eighties, Sears and IBM were forming a joint venture called Prodigy to capture online consumer services. If you remember Prodigy, you are definitely a member of the baby boom generation! The Prodigy development team wanted to include an online brokerage service—the first of its kind. Sears already had an affiliated brokerage house, Dean Witter Reynolds, but they declined to participate, deeming the venture too risky. Pershing was contacted, and after an explanation of the opportunity from one of his lieutenants, Dick said, "Why not?" This "why not?" turned into DLJ Direct, which had a $4 billion market valuation at its peak.

It's important to acknowledge that this was an educated "why not." Under Dick's leadership, DLJ had already become one of the largest and most efficient securities trading houses. This had occurred as a result of Dick's leadership in buying and developing the Pershing business. Ultimately, Pershing's processing capability provided a strong framework for moving into the online business. So "why not," indeed? As usual, while others in the industry were shying away, Dick Pechter was saying yes.

Dick is insistent that he made many mistakes, and that much of his success occurred only because of what he learned from his failures. This is undoubtedly true up to a point, but it was Dick's openness to trying new things that made all the difference. In fact, Dick will admit that he made it a practice to "just say yes and trust my team."

By his 55th birthday in 1999, Dick truly reached the pinnacle of his career. Several forces came together that got him thinking about what should be next. Personally, the 24/7 nature of the investment business had begun taking its toll. He had always loved his work, but now some days he just found he didn't have the same zest for it. He began to find himself out of step with younger colleagues. Recognizing that Wall Street has always been a young man's game, he decided that maybe it was time to get out of the way of the next generation. So he set his retirement in motion, resolving to retire in January of the year 2000.

Almost 10 years earlier, DLJ had moved part of its operation to Jersey City. At that time, in the interest of corporate civic involvement, they had begun a mentoring program in the local inner city high school. Dick was thunderstruck walking into that school through metal detectors and armed guards. What a challenge it must be for those kids to learn! He never stopped thinking about it.

As he neared the date of his retirement, the thought of teaching began to emerge. He'd been a math major at Yale, loved the theory and discipline of it, but had been discouraged by his professors from pursuing his PhD, since he wasn't "good enough" to teach. So he headed to Harvard for an MBA instead and the rest is history.

Now he realized he was free to choose to teach if he wanted to. In his usual style Dick said, "Why not?" He applied to Teach for America and was accepted. Less than six months after his retirement he began a rigorous training program in which most participants were less than half his age. By the time the year was out he was in a Jersey City high school classroom.

Dick taught for over five years in high school, middle school, and ultimately community college. Today, now again retired—this time from his teaching career—he remains passionate about education, still sitting on the board of Teach for America. "Teaching was one of the most humbling experiences of my life. I learned quickly that my preconceived ideas about how to fix education crumbled in the face of day-to-day reality. The kids taught me so much about life. And so, why not?"

When will you say "why not"?

Toolkit

We have included examples of the worksheets and tools you will need to implement in this chapter:

1. Balance Sheet for Financial Capital
2. Balance Sheet for Human Capital
3. Possible Spending Categories

If you go to our website at www.lntyee.com you can register to download copies of the worksheets and exercises.

Worksheet 1: Balance Sheet for Financial Capital

Date at: _____

	Assets	Liabilities	Comments/Actions
Liquid Assets			
Retirement Assets			
Other Investment and Business Assets			
Personal Assets			
TOTALS:			////////////////
		NET WORTH:	

Directions:

- List all your personal assets and liabilities according to their category.
- Draw down totals.
- Net worth is equal to total assets minus total liabilities.

Worksheet 2: Balance Sheet for Human Capital

Date: _____

	Assets (+)	Liabilities (−)	Comments/Actions
Well-Being			
• Health			
• Peace of Mind			
• Lifestyle			
• Learning/Growth			
Relationships			
• Spouse or Partner			
• Immediate Family			
• Extended Family			
• Friends			
• Business Colleagues			
Fulfillment			
• Work			
• Creativity			
• Community			
• Philanthropy			
• Politics			
Legacy			
• Immediate Family			
• Extended Family			
• Friends			
• Community			
• Profession/Business			
• Politics			
TOTALS:			

Directions:

- Use a straightforward plus or minus system to score.
- Plus signs go in the Assets column while minus signs go in the Liability column.
- On some things you may use multiple plus signs or minus signs. On others you may choose to leave it blank as not applicable.
- Add any item that matters to you.
- Do you have more pluses than minuses?

Worksheet 3: Possible Spending Categories

Use this list as a starting place to determine the best categories to fit your spending.

Home
- Rent or mortgage payment
- Utilities
- Insurance
- Property taxes
- Maintenance
- Improvements

Food
- Groceries
- Eating out
- Entertaining

Health
- Insurance
- Out of pocket
- Fitness

Automobiles
- Lease/payment
- Gas
- Repairs and maintenance
- Licensing
- Insurance

Clothing
Personal Care

Pets

- Food
- Vet
- Grooming/boarding

Entertainment/Leisure

- Hobbies
- Travel
- Sports
- Books/movies

Family Responsibilities

- Alimony
- Child support
- Tuition payments

Charity

- Donations
- Volunteer expenses

Miscellaneous

Note: Property taxes are included here, income taxes are not. We recommend looking at income taxes separately as you consider future income sources.

CHAPTER 8

Know Who You Are

We have found that an essential part of knowing where you are is knowing *who* you are. *Who* you are has clearly been forged over many years through many and varied experiences. We have no doubt that you have had both triumphs and tragedies. Where you are today is a tapestry woven from that past. It is by understanding this that you can best determine how to go forward. It is something of a paradox that you must look backward over your life to see what matters to go forward. But there you are.

Recognizing the Crucible

Most of us, as we engage in this process, have a tendency to focus on the "marquee" events in our lives. These are the things that everyone thinks of as headliners—births, deaths, graduations, marriages, divorce, and so on. But for what we're suggesting here you need to get behind those headlines to understand how your past continues to drive you today. One of our favorite authors on this topic is Bill George. His book *True North* speaks eloquently about events he calls crucibles, the things that happen to you that change your life forever.

> A crucible can be triggered by events such as confronting a difficult situation at work, receiving critical feedback, or losing your job. Or it may result from a painful personal experience such as divorce, illness, or the death of a loved one.[1]

---

[1] Bill George with Peter Sims, *True North* (San Francisco: Jossey-Bass, 2007), p. 46.

Your crucible tests you to the core of your being. It forces you to look at yourself, examine your character and your values in a new light, and to come to grips with who you are. Viewed in retrospect, your crucible may become the defining experience in your life, even if you do not recognize it when you are in the middle of the experience.[2]

George based his view of the importance of understanding your personal history on many interviews with CEOs. He found a high correlation between the CEO's level of self-understanding and long-term business success. We see this phenomenon in our work as well. When it comes to personal financial success, our experience with the families and entrepreneurs we serve always tells the same tale. Self-reflection, even when it's painful, yields better results.

Facing the Questions

Even in early interviews with new clients, we start asking questions about personal history with the goal of uncovering personal priorities. At the end of this chapter we have provided you with some exercises similar to that early interview experience. If you have any doubts about whether this would be valuable for you, grab something to write with and answer these three questions. No need to write essays; a few key words will do.

- What are you most proud of?
- What in life would you like a do-over for?
- What has made you sad or frightened?

Over and over again we find that these kinds of questions turn over some very interesting personal rocks. You might be surprised what you find underneath. Sometimes these rocks have been untouched for years. Often these questions elicit childhood memories that drive adult passions—like Kaycee and her first dog or like Bob and his penchant for fairness. Or they may resurface regrets: "I didn't spend enough time with my children when they were very young." Perhaps sadness or fear emerges. Many a person's commitment to end homelessness or help at-risk youth comes from a depth of personal experience. You don't know what's there until you ask yourself. So what did you find?

---

[2] Bill George, Andrew McLean, and Nick Craig, *Finding Your True North* (San Francisco: Jossey-Bass, 2008), p. 36.

Back to the Future

We suggest you begin your look backward by preparing a personal history matrix. This is simply a schedule that notes key life stages (like early childhood) and asks you questions about what was going on in your life at those times. As you look at each stage, the matrix suggests you jot down recollections:

• Name a milestone (or a few of them) for this point in your life.
• When I think about this time in my life, my most vivid memory is . . .
• Something I learned then that is still useful to me today is . . .

It is helpful to put this matrix together before you take a stab at the longer questions posed in the Your Life in Retrospect exercise at the end of the chapter. It is a great mental preparation for the reflection required to complete those essays.

Seriously, Try This Now

We know what you're thinking: "I already know myself pretty well; I don't need to bother doing this." It is likely nothing could be further from the truth. Kaycee's experience is particularly instructive here, and a great example of why you might want to make time for this. While she had used these techniques with clients for years, she never bothered to use them on herself until after the cancer gave her a wake-up call. She found the results fascinating and very useful. In fact, the book you're reading would not exist if she had not done that self-reflection. We can say with some certainty that even those with a very high level of self-awareness can profit from further reflection, particularly when they reach a point of major transition. That's all we're asking you to do here.

And When You Have a Partner

We know we said it's about you this time—and it is. But if you are part of a committed relationship, taking into consideration the values, goals, and desires of your partner becomes part of the task. The tricky part can be getting the dialogue going.

When it comes to what's next in life, those that care about you often want to give you "space." They may attempt to be Switzerland and stay completely neutral. You get comments like "Whatever you think best, dear. It's your life." But assuming you are not planning to split up any time soon, it's impossible to create your own game plan without some sense of what really matters to your partner. You don't need them to tell you what to do, but you do want them to help you put the boundaries on the playing field.

In our experience this can be complicated. In relationships of long standing, sometimes you assume you know what the other person is thinking or what they want. After all, you have had years or decades to figure this out, right? Wrong. When big transitions are on the horizon, everything is up for grabs.

Now more than ever, you want to check any preconceived notions about your partner at the door. You can seize this as an opportunity to connect about what matters most. Earlier we suggested that you have some fairly deep conversations with yourself. At this point we are suggesting that you expand the circle to include your significant other. Here are a few suggestions:

Use This Book—It's always interesting and usually valuable for both spouses to do the personal history exercises we outline in this chapter. You can prepare them separately and then compare notes. We often do this as part of our legacy planning process. Clients tell us (sometimes years later) that they learned things about each other that helped them make better decisions on many levels.

You may even want to give your partner their own copy of this book so they can hash through this at their own pace and in their own style. When one person in a committed relationship is facing transition, the other is often equally affected and may also face some surprising changes. Planning together and in tandem never hurts and may be very helpful.

Take a Road Trip—Many people (Kaycee and Bob for sure) find some of the best conversations they ever have with their spouses are those in the car. Go figure. Maybe it is being together in the moving box? Maybe it's the thrill of the open road? It's hard to say. But what is definitely true is that in the car you seem to be able to have the time and space to go deep on the issues. And that's what we're looking for here. Now is clearly a time to go deep. So schedule a road trip! We will arm you with proposed questions to get your conversation kick-started.

Here are a few questions that we love; there are more at the end of the chapter:

- What do you care enough about that you would argue with someone over it at a very nice dinner party?
- How do others know what matters to you? Can you name the ways you walk your talk?
- Describe what success looks like for our children. What do you want most for them?
- Let's say you have been dead 10 years. Are you still making a difference in people's lives? How? Or do you even care?
- What is a perfect day like? Provide vivid details.
- What worries you enough to keep you awake at night?
- What energizes you each day? Or could?

We could go on and on with this stuff, but you get the drift. You'll note that these questions are not directly about money. Rather, they are about the human capital factors—well-being, relationships, fulfillment, and legacy—that should determine how you deploy your financial capital. And they flow right into how you'll ultimately define your personal mission.

You'll also note that these are not personal history questions. We think the personal history piece is best done individually, using the tools at the end of this chapter and then comparing notes. Rather, these questions set the stage for the work you'll be doing next—figuring out where you want to go.

There's no question that having these kinds of conversations with your partner solidifies that you are a team. And when change is on the horizon you know, better than most people, that a strong team is what carries you through.

Flow

As you go through the exercises, there is one particular bias that we'd like you to be aware of. We expect that your chief motivation in doing the work that we have suggested here is the desire to figure out what's next in your own life. You will find the same exercises are useful for other things, even estate planning. But the main game right now is what is next for *you*. For that reason we are going to ask you to pay attention to a thing called *flow*.

Flow is something that has clearly been a part of human experience for millennia, but has only recently been studied. The term *flow* was created by Mihaly Csikszentmihalyi to describe his area of interest as a psychological researcher and became the name of his famous book on the subject. (We've been told by those who know these things that you pronounce his name My-holly Chicks-sent-my-holly.)

Csikszentmihalyi asserts that those with the happiest lives are those who have what he calls optimal experiences, and these experiences are not what you might think. To quote from *Flow*:

> . . . the best moments in our lives are not the passive receptive relaxing times—although such experiences can also be enjoyable, if we have worked hard to attain them. The best moments usually occur when a person's body or mind is stretched to its limits in a voluntary effort to accomplish something difficult and worthwhile.[3]

You can see why understanding these things about yourself might offer great insight into what you should be doing next in your life, assuming living with joy is on your to-do list. Csikszentmihalyi further describes a state that humans can achieve when they are most in the grip of these optimal experiences. He defines the concept of flow as:

> . . . the state in which people are so involved in an activity that nothing else seems to matter; the experience itself is so enjoyable that people will do it even at great cost, for the sheer sake of doing it.[4]

So as you work through the exercises, keep in mind that understanding what moments have truly been your best moments and what activities place you in that state of flow are exactly what you're looking for. Who doesn't want to maximize optimal experiences in their lives and the lives of the people they love? So ask yourself, when am I in the flow?

So Enough Touchy-Feely Already?

In our culture, it is still difficult to talk about these things. We don't like to get touchy-feely, even though we may be delighted to witness it in others, à la Oprah. Yet you must get clarity about these things if you want to create a context for building a true Wealth Regeneration discipline, the kind of discipline that can carry you through your lifetime and possibly help your loved ones after you're gone. We are definitely suggesting here that the only thing you can truly count on is change. In the face of change you need to be able to get back to the bedrock of who you are and what matters most to you. These exercises don't create your bedrock; that's already there. The point is

---

[3] Mihaly Csikszentmihalyi, *Flow: The Psychology of Optimal Experience* (New York: Harper-Collins, 1990), p. 3.
[4] Ibid, p. 4.

to help you uncover it and make it a more intentional part of your decision making along the way.

So even if you're one of those people who say "I hate the vision thing," stick with us here. As we roll along the way you will see more and more evidence of why that vision thing will carry the day in the face of constant change, no matter what kind of change life brings you.

PROFILE: PETER NOSTRAND

Peter Nostrand has loved music his entire life. He grew up in a family of talented musicians, although no one in his family had made it their liveli-hood. He recalls family concert evenings when his grandmother would do things like transpose a piece of music into a different key—all on the fly and by sight—to make it easier for young voices to sing. So Peter comes by his talent naturally. As a kid, Peter had two passions—baseball and the pia-no—but neither was to become his career. After graduating from Amherst and a few years teaching French in a girl's school in Middleburg, Virginia, reality set in. If Peter was to support his young family, a real job was required. So Peter entered the world of banking in Richmond, Virginia as a management trainee for what was then known as United Virginia Bank.

Peter, like many in the baby-boom generation, is very forthright in acknowledging that his career in banking came out of necessity rather than a passion for finance. Yet he threw himself into it. "I'm the old ste-reotype," Peter says. "I just like to work and will probably die in motion."

In this new life, there was little time for music. Peter adopted the practice of being the first person there in the morning and the last person to leave at night. His tenacity and drive paid off. By 1995 he had risen to become the CEO of the bank's greater Washington region. Eleven years later, he elected to retire.

Peter says that he retired with two thoughts, that he would be able to start playing the piano again, and he would be able to travel; a welcome relief from going to loan committee meetings. What could be better than that? Despite the brave façade, he said that inside he was terrified. Like others in the CEO role, he had become his job. He truly enjoyed it, had been doing it for many years, and he really didn't know how to be any-thing else. So in retirement he was heading off into unmapped territory.

About six months into his retirement he began waking up at night with melodies in his head. As a youth he had learned how to score music from his dad, so he began writing these melodies down. Quickly what had been a trickle of melodies became a flood. And a new career was born.

(continued)

Peter threw himself into composing with his usual intensity. He began to reach out to anyone and everyone he could think of that had any connection to music to seek advice. "You would be surprised who you can get to," he says, "if you are willing just to call them up on the phone and ask for help." Along the way he studied at Oxford and engaged the Czech Philharmonic in Prague to perform some of his pieces. If you go online to www.Peternostrand.com you can hear samples of Peter's music. He has won awards for his work, although he's still working on how to create commercial success. He describes his style as somewhere between Haydn and Hollywood, and he has recently wandered into country music. At this writing, six of his songs are being circulated in country music circles for possible recording.

When asked if there was anything he wanted a do-over for, Peter responds quickly, "Nothing, really." When asked if he wished he had pursued music early in life, he is clear that the answer is no. "I enjoyed my career and all the experiences it provided me as well as the good life it provided for my family. It has allowed me to compose, and to engage musicians to perform my work, be it classical, country, or big screen, and on absolutely my own terms. That works for me." He adds, "Besides, retirement is not about sitting around waiting for the end. It should represent a new beginning, a new challenge, and new opportunities to grow. Everyone has a dream. Just find it and go for it."

When will you listen to your dream?

Toolkit

We have included examples of the worksheets and tools you will need to implement in this chapter:

1. Food for Thought
2. Personal History Matrix
3. Your Life in Retrospect
4. More Great Questions for the Car

Worksheet 1: Food for Thought

1. Write down something you are proud of:

_____

_____

_____

2. Write down something you would like a "do over" for:

_____

_____

_____

3. Write down something that made you sad or frightened:

_____

_____

_____

Worksheet 2: Personal History Matrix

AGE	Name a milestone (or a few) for this point in your life	When I think about this time of my life, the first thing that comes to mind is:	What is my most vivid memory?	Something I learned then, that is still useful to me today:
Early Childhood				
Middle Childhood				
Teenage Years				
College and Launch				
Young Adulthood				
Mid Life				
Today				

Worksheet 3: Your Life in Retrospect

1. When you look at your milestones, are there any that jump out at you as particularly worthwhile?

_____

_____

2. Do you have milestones for both your business life and your personal life?

_____

_____

3. What times (or events or milestones) made you the happiest? Why? Are they still part of your life?

_____

_____

4. If you could live your life all over again, what would you do differently?

_____

_____

5. When do you experience _flow_ (that is, losing yourself so much in an activity that you lose track of time)?

_____

_____

6. Have you experienced a crucible? What was it?

_____

_____

_____

Worksheet 4: More Great Questions for the Car (or Date Night or on a Beach . . .)

- What gives you peace of mind?
- What do you want to preserve besides wealth?
- Does your lifestyle reflect your values?
- What are your priorities at this stage in life?
- What is important to you?
- What are your core values?
- What might others say is your claim to fame?

- How much do you want to tell our children about our wealth?
- What do you want most for our children?
- How do you define an appropriate financial inheritance for our children?
- What is your own experience with a financial inheritance? What type of experience do you want our children to have?
- Do you think you have a good plan in place now? If not, why not?
- Is there anything in your present financial plan that frustrates you or is getting in the way?
- How comfortable are you at ceding control to others?
- How much do you want to do at this point in your life?

CHAPTER 9

Know Where You Want to Go

It is now time to look forward. At this juncture, if you've completed the tasks we've asked of you, you should have a pretty good sense of:

- Where you stand with both your human capital and financial capital.
- The real parameters of what it costs to live your lifestyle.
- Where you might fit on the wealth continuum.

From the review of your personal history you've also established some important context for looking into the future. We'd say you're ready to pull yourself up to 30,000 feet and take a look at what you want and where you truly would like to go. In business terms, it is time to create a mission and a vision. Yet there is one last task we propose before you go there.

Embracing the Endgame

While it may seem uncomfortable, we have now reached the inevitable point in our conversation where we must talk about the end of the story—life expectancy—and we mean yours. Even if your grandfather lived to be 98 and you are highly confident in your own genetic ability to beat the odds, there will be an endgame. There always is. And recognizing it makes planning for what's next even more vivid.

We have found that penciling out the details of what you expect to happen over the next 0 to 50 years kind of puts all it in perspective. Think of this as akin to putting Post-it notes on some kind of project chart on the wall. Only one of those Post-it notes will say "I exit." To make this as easy as

81

FIGURE 9.1 Your Life Timeline

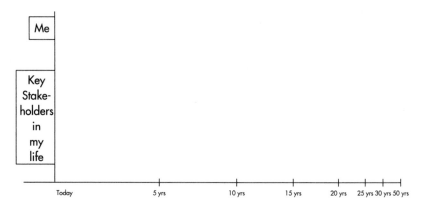

possible, we actually use a chart approach that we call the Life Timeline (see Figure 9.1). Here's what it looks like for starters.

It is most similar to that kind of project management chart on which you list multiple elements of a project and what should happen at points along the way. You know at the get-go that everything on it is somewhat moveable, but you get them down to provide a bird's-eye view of the whole project. You use these charts to identify bottlenecks and opportunities, and then negotiate what needs to be moved. In this case the whole project is your life and all the people in it.

Figure 9.2 is an example of one filled out with the ages and possible milestones of a hypothetical family.

FIGURE 9.2 Timeline with Ages and Milestones

	Today	5 yrs	10 yrs	15 yrs	20 yrs	25 yrs 30 yrs 50 yrs
Me	62 Retire	Sell home move into condo — Around the world trip	67	Sell — vacation home?	72 We move into — a life care facility	78
Anne	60	65	70	75		
Kids:						
Michael	36	Wants to start a business	41	46	51	
Moira	28	Gets married?	33	Help with first house 38	43	
Parents:						
John	78	83	Out-of-home care?	88	?	
Shirley	80	85		90	?	
Grandkids:			More grandkids?			
Dean	4	9	14 Graduate high school	19	Complete college	
Charlie	6	11	16 Graduate high school	21	Complete college	

FIGURE 9.3   Your Life Timeline

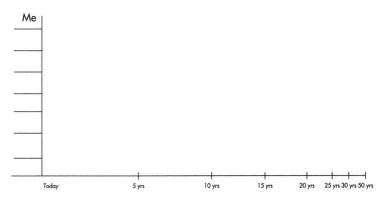

Directions: Identify key stakeholders in your life and list them on the vertical axis. Then jot their ages at various points in time. Once that is done, fill in with notes of possible life events and milestones.

As you can imagine, this Life Timeline provides the impetus for some important discussions. It makes visual and concrete the fact that life moves quickly and sets the stage for determining priorities. Aging parents? Children who need help today? Grandchildren who will be all grown up before you know it? The Life Timeline lays it all out.

To put together your own Life Timeline we have provided a detailed worksheet at the end of the chapter. You can see what it looks like in Figure 9.3.

The first task is to determine the stakeholders in your life. You'll see that the chart already has you at the top of the list, but who or what else might you include? Your human capital balance sheet provides many clues. And entities like the business you founded or a charity you strongly support might be stakeholders too. List those stakeholders down the side of the chart.

In the example in Figure 9.2, we have listed the usual suspects: spouse, children, parents, and grandkids. There is no right or wrong as to whom or what you list and how. Though we do know most spouses expect to be on the list and at the top of the list! You don't need to include every possible stakeholder, say, your employees or your Scout troop: This list is for the biggies. It should include those with whom you can reasonably expect to maintain long-term relationships.

On the timeline you will chart important expected events over time. Begin with your age at different points, then add ages of the others at key points as well. Then chart the possible events—births, deaths (yes, make a guess), graduations, business sales, and so on. If you are squeamish about actually pinpointing life expectancy, particularly for others, consider using question marks. If you look back at the example in Figure 9.2 you'll see a question mark used to denote ages individuals may or may not attain.

The timeline itself is on what is called a logarithmic scale. That simply leaves more space for events likely to be sooner—and less for those likely to be later. This log scale fits better with how most of us think and plan about future events. The sooner something is likely to happen, the more attention you are likely to want to give it—given that the farther out you go, the more uncertain things get. It's human nature and the lifeline accommodates that.

At this point you can start dropping in some more detailed personal items—like what year you thought you might retire or qualify to run the New York Marathon. Let your imagination flow a bit. Have you always said that someday you'll sail around the world? Consider putting that into the timeline.

And then it hits you as you begin looking at all the critical dates and personal milestones for yourself and the people you care for. The sense that life is short is more palpable. There is a poignancy about it. As you look at it you may discover a new urgency about some of the things you have been meaning to do. That's the power of looking at a timeline of your life.

In looking at our example in Figure 9.2 you can imagine this guy asking himself, "Hey, those grandkids aren't getting any younger! When exactly am I taking them (pick one) on a real camping trip . . . to see the old family farm . . . to Washington, D.C. to see the Declaration of Independence or maybe the White House . . . just fishing?" This is exactly the kind of thing this exercise is designed to bring up. It's rather the point of it all. So as you put your timeline together, be sure to listen carefully to what it is telling you.

Now the Life Timeline is not the answer to the *know where you want to go* part of our process. But it helps create the strongest possible context for crafting the answer. All along the way we've emphasized that ultimately you are at the center of the Wealth Regeneration wheel, and that remains true. Yet as you explore the bigger questions of what's next, reminders of each aspect of your wealth—but most specifically the wealth of your relationships—is helpful.

Getting Strategic

In every strategic plan someone writes about a business you see the terms *mission*, *vision*, and *values*. Because Wealth Regeneration is fundamentally strategic planning for the rest of your life, we are going to suggest that you do that here as well, only in a different way. In some respects you'll find this easier than in a business context. Look on the bright side; there will be no need to wordsmith this with a fussy committee or create a laminated wall poster! And you don't have to show it to anyone, although you may choose to.

We suggest that you formulate a thing we call a *purpose statement*. This is very much like a business's mission statement but goes a bit further because we ask you to be clear about the *why*. We will also ask you to craft a type of vision. This will be less global in scope than most business visions but still will speak tangibly to what you hope to see in the next phase of your life.

Trust us; we will make this as painless as possible.

Your Purpose

We never cease to be amazed at how often strategic plans for businesses ignore purpose. They say things like: "To be the most profitable business like us anywhere in the globe." Yet they ignore the essential question of why. Not that profit isn't a good thing, mind you! We are all about profit, but there still needs to be a *why*. More profits to pay out to the shareholders? More profits to reward key employees? More profits to fuel new innovations? The answer in a business setting could be all of the above. (Though most successful businesses choose one key focus.) But you get our point.

Here's another one of our favorites: "To amaze and delight our customers daily." It's the same problem, not that amazement and delight are not awesome things, but why? If you think about the best business mission statements you've heard, they are short, sweet, and loaded with purpose.

For individuals, we believe the element of purpose in the statement is even more critical. Think about it this way—if you don't answer the classic questions, Who cares? So what? What's in it for me?—how can you use the statement as a measure or guidepost for what you want to do next? The "what's in it for me" piece can actually be very altruistic, but still has got to be there. Otherwise the statement is incomplete.

What are the hallmarks of a useful statement? We believe it must be short and easily remembered—what use is it if you have to look it up all the time? The language needs to be meaningful to you. Since this statement is not for publication, phrase it in whatever way most resonates for you. This statement should have a timelessness about it; it should never feel like a to-do list. In fact, it's okay if it looks like the sort of thing that might be cross-stitched on a sofa pillow.

Give it a try:

My purpose is . . . _____

_____

_____

Not easy, is it? Here are a few examples, and yes, they are from real people, but we are not telling you who. Most people tend to be a private about their purpose.

- "Use my mind to help others solve important and meaningful problems."
- "Give everyone I touch a chance to thrive, because that's how I thrive."
- "Experience as many things as possible with as many people as possible to form the deepest relationships possible."
- "Use my abundance to help others create their own abundance."
- "Wake up every day with joy and optimism and spread it around."
- "Never stop learning."

Don't be surprised if this is incredibly difficult. Most of us are intimidated when we are asked to choose just one thing, so plan on giving yourself some time to work on it. And here are a few tips to help.

- Write about other things first—at the end of this chapter we have included a list of questions about discovering your passions. This is Worksheet 2. Give yourself a chance to write the answers to these questions. And while you are writing, take care to write as fast as you possibly can and see what emerges. There's a good body of research that suggests that writing fast releases creative thinking.
- Phone a friend—this is not just a game show technique (whether it's "Cash Cab" or "Who Wants to Be a Millionaire"). A phone call with a friend can be the perfect kick right where you need it. Don't expect a friend to tell you the answer—although we do know of cases where this has happened—but do expect them to help you engage your mind around the issue, perhaps in ways you haven't even considered. Don't have any friends that you feel comfortable talking to about the purpose of your life? Head right back to that pesky human capital balance sheet. You have work to do. If you have been avoiding filling out the human capital information (and we know who you are), now may be the time.
- Just let it sit—there's no perfect way to figure all these things out. Sometimes you just need to let it sit on the back burner of your brain until something

comes to you. Sometimes it's best just to keep working on other aspects of Wealth Regeneration. And sometimes it's best just to clean out your desk. Suddenly you'll see your purpose embedded in what you're doing.

And finally, remember that for most of us our purpose is not something we decide all of a sudden. It is more a natural outgrowth of who we are. You may have been living your purpose all your life and just never have written it down. At a time like this, where you are sorting out what's next for the rest of your life, actually writing it down is helpful. You can do this on Worksheet 3 found at the end of the chapter.

We believe it's likely that even during your business life you probably conducted yourself in a manner consistent with your purpose. Otherwise you would not have been a successful leader. We all know you can be a successful phony over short periods of time, but over the long haul people figure you out. Authenticity is a must-have attribute for long-term success. We refuse to believe that someone goes from being a draconian boss to an empowering flower child just because they "found" their purpose. Just doesn't happen.

In its way this is simply a "back to the future" exercise. Look back over your life and ask yourself what you see. There will surely be a purpose in there somewhere. It's time for you to claim it.

Now for That Vision Thing

Every sound strategy has a vision for how things turn out. What you want out of a personal strategic vision is much less precise than in the business world. In a business vision you typically see financial or positional targets like profitability or market share. In your own life, vision still will be most useful if it is fairly concrete and detailed, yet the targets for measurement will be looser. You will have some specific milestones combined with other things that are more about the general state of affairs. That's why personal vision is more descriptive. As you read it, you are able to get a picture in your mind of just how it might be. The more vivid and evocative the details, the better. Because personal vision is just that, personal, there are many ways to formulate one. However, we have found two techniques that work for many people—writing a letter or creating a schedule. Here is how they work.

- Writing a letter—With this technique you write an imaginary letter (or e-mail or Facebook post) to a good friend that you might send at some point in the future. In it you describe how things are for you. It is the kind of missive that you send to friends who live at a distance to catch them up on your life. What would you want to be able to tell them?

- Creating a schedule—Here you simply lay out the schedule for an imaginary day in the future. We are certain you will still have a calendar to manage whatever comes next. When do you get up? What appointments are scheduled? Who are you spending time with? How does the day end?

Now these two techniques might sound a little corny, but they are substantially less daunting than sitting down to a blank sheet of paper or computer screen and saying to yourself "Write vision now." And they actually get you to the same outcome. What you finally want in your vision is enough detail to be able to ask yourself "Am I getting there from here?"

How Does It Look from the Top of the Mountain?

What you are working on right now, purpose, passion, and vision, will become the primary driving forces behind your plan. Looking at life expectancy in a clear-eyed way creates urgency for most of us. Combine that with acknowledging that you are living on purpose and have a vision for how that plays out in your life, and you have momentum for forward motion. It is all about keeping that wheel turning.

PROFILE: BOB BUNTING

Bob Bunting is the former CEO of Moss Adams, one of the largest CPA firms in the United States, headquartered on the West Coast. Under his 23 years of leadership, the firm grew from seven offices and $16 million in revenue to 19 offices with over $280 million in revenue at the point of his retirement. Today he remains affiliated with Moss Adams in a kind of roving ambassador role. His most recent focus has been on the importance of a level playing field for global commerce when it comes to financial regulation.

You can't understand Bob Bunting unless you first understand a bit about how he grew up in Grangeville, Idaho. Grangeville was and is the kind of American small town that is said to have character. It was the kind of town where everyone pulls together to get things done; the kind of community where if you care about something, it is expected that you give of your time and talent to make your community a better place. And the kind of place where you learn that if you expect to do well yourself, it is wise to help others along the way. Bob never forgot these lessons.

Bob was a natural leader early on. He says he always wanted to run things, and wasn't satisfied unless he rose to the top of every activity. He also says his parents often worried that he was "too big for his britches." His earliest lesson in leadership was on a Boy Scout winter camping trip on the Clearwater River. He convinced two other Scouts that they should sneak out of camp to hike up the adjacent mountain. Did the scoutmaster know? Of course not! Needless to say, a couple of hours later Bob and his loyal adherents were hopelessly lost on the mountainside. When the other two boys looked at him and said "What are we going to do?" Bob admits that he panicked and burst into tears, a true leadership moment. But they all got down the mountain safely and back into camp without anyone being the wiser.

Eager for financial independence, Bob decided to study accounting at the University of Idaho, which had a top-notch program. From there he was recruited to Price Waterhouse as a consultant and then within a few years recruited by Moss Adams to head their consulting group. By age 27 he had become a partner of Moss Adams. And by age 34 he was the CEO.

Throughout his career Bob has had a history of being thrown into the deep end of the pool and thriving. His leadership role at Moss Adams was no exception. He attributes this to a series of great mentors.

Bob's 23-year tenure as the CEO of Moss Adams is an unusually long one by any standard. He attributes this to reinventing himself and the job about every five years. Bob asked one of his mentors, John Van Horn, "Do you ever get bored?" John replied, "Yes, I do, and that's what always causes me to do something interesting." This advice was particularly invaluable as Bob approached retirement.

After so many years at the helm, he recognized that he was running out of reinventions. He saw that he was becoming impatient and wasn't giving people the time to develop that they needed. In short, he says he saw himself morphing into "a cranky old man." It was clearly time to do something different—and it had to be interesting. Because of the success that they had achieved together, his partners wanted him to stay on with Moss Adams in some capacity, so his new ambassador role was created. But what should he be doing?

Echoing his Grangeville heritage, Bob had always given back to his professional community as a CPA. He had been active in the American

(continued)

Institute of CPAs since the 1970s. Believing that his profession was only as good as its bottom rung, he had helped pioneer peer review of CPA firms and served as the chairman of the Board of Examiners, traveling the country to explain the new rules and opportunities to practitioners. He went on to chair other committees and task forces for the AICPA over the years.

Now this professional life was about to provide the something new and interesting that Bob required. In 2004 Bob went on to chair the American Institute of CPAs—one of the largest professional organizations of its type with over 340,000 members. Then he moved on in 2007 to become the president of IFAC, the International Federation of Accountants, traveling the world promoting high standards. Bob remains involved with both the AICPA and IFAC today.

Why stay focused on his profession? Bob puts it well: "I believe strongly in the power of leverage. I always ask people, what can you leverage?" He takes it a step further, "In retirement, I might have pounded nails for Habitat for Humanity and I would have enjoyed it, but it felt selfish. I'm not the greatest nail pounder. Shouldn't I be giving back in ways that use all my skills? That's what I mean by leverage."

Now that his work on global business regulation is winding down, his newest project is leading a task force for the AICPA looking at how to measure and report on the sustainability of an enterprise. Here he is leveraging all his skills, he continues "to do something interesting," and, just as he learned in Grangeville, he continues to give of his time and talent to make his community a better place.

What lessons have you learned?

Tookit

We have included here examples of the worksheets and tools you will need to implement in this chapter:

1. Your Life Timeline
2. Discovering Your Passions
3. Your Purpose
4. Letter to a Friend
5. Schedule for a Future Day

Worksheet 1: Your Life Timeline

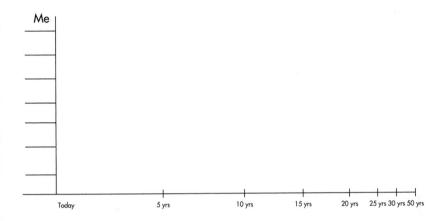

Directions: Identify key stakeholders in your life and list them on the vertical axis. Then jot their ages at various points in time. Once that is done, fill in with notes of possible life events and milestones.

Worksheet 2: Discovering Your Passions

1. If you had unlimited time, talents, and resources, what would you choose to do?

_____

_____

_____

_____

_____

2. What kinds of things energize you to get up in the morning?

_____

_____

_____

_____

_____

_____

3. Though you may have dismissed such thoughts many times before for various reasons, are there things you feel you really should do? What are they?

_____

_____

_____

_____

_____

_____

4. If you only had 30 days left to live but had perfect health, unlimited energy, and money, what would you spend your last 30 days doing?

_____

_____

_____

_____

_____

5. If you could make the world a better place to live in just one way, what would it be?

_____

_____

_____

_____

_____

Worksheet 3: Your Purpose

My purpose is:

_____

_____

_____

_____

_____

_____

_____

Worksheet 4: Letter to a Friend

Dear _____,

_____

_____

_____

_____

_____

_____

_____

Instructions: Describe your desired life in as much detail as possible.

- What are you doing?
- Where are you?
- Who are you with?
- What is it like?

Worksheet 5: Schedule for a Future Day

MORNING: _____

_____
_____
_____
_____
_____

NOON: _____

_____
_____
_____
_____
_____

EVENING: _____

_____
_____
_____
_____
_____

Instructions: Create the schedule for your desired day.

- What are you doing?
- Where are you?
- Who are you with?
- What is it like?

CHAPTER 10

What to Do to Get There from Here

Now, it's time for you to turn all this into a real plan, and one that works. We have all seen it—thoughtful strategic plans that go nowhere due to lack of execution. Failure to execute is unfortunately very common in today's competitive world.

So when it comes to your own game plan for Wealth Regeneration, incorporating a framework for execution just makes sense. Otherwise what we have been doing here is nothing more than an entertaining exercise.

You can begin by actually capturing your thinking in a personal strategic plan document, putting it in writing in some form or fashion, since things committed to writing are more likely to be accomplished. But it takes more than just recording your ideas. Our experience tells us that successful execution of any kind of strategy comes from three constituents—keeping it simple, making it actionable, and assigning clear accountability. We will show you how to make these a natural part of your plan.

Keeping It Real

When it comes to putting together planning documents, this is undoubtedly not your first rodeo. You know what kind of documents work best for you and your style, and that is exactly the kind of document you should have. We have been doing this for a while, so we will make some suggestions based on what we have seen work over the years with our clients. But if you've got a better way to put this document together, go to it. And we'd love it if you e-mail us your ideas.

Here are some fundamentals about the kind of documents we think work best:

- Simplicity—This is one you know in your heart. No one needs a big fancy detailed document when it comes to this stuff. In fact, those kinds of documents seem to be the most prone to failure. Rather, you want to aspire to the short and sweet—think "my life on a cocktail napkin," if you get our drift. Of course, nowadays this has become "my life on my iPad." The kind of simple document we like to see uses clear language and doesn't worry too much about sentence structure. In fact, it is possible to do this entirely in bullet points. Brief is good.
- Ease of action—The test of our desired simplicity is whether or not you can put the plan into action. Is it obvious what to do? Can you articulate the next steps? Is it easy to digest, or do you need to break things into bite-size chunks? Whose responsibility is it, anyway? Do you know what success looks like? Can some third party look at what you said, compared to what you have done, and make an informed judgment?
- Clear accountability—We have said throughout that the key to Wealth Regeneration is feedback. You need reality checks all along the way. You can't adapt to changing times if you are not looking whatever is happening right in the eye and comparing it to what you expected. That's the secret of staying on track. That's exactly what a GPS tells you. Where are you? Are you still headed in the right direction? Have you done what you said you would do? Has life thrown you a detour? Or has a new opportunity cropped up that you want to seriously consider? You must have a thoughtful approach to holding yourself and those around you account-able in order to move forward.

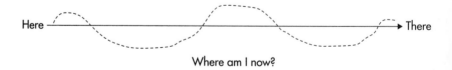

Where am I now?

So what would a plan that embraces simplicity, ease of action, and accountability look like? We have some suggestions, as you might expect.

We will actually give you a detailed outline (see Worksheet 1 at the end of the chapter). Here is the overall flow of the document:

- Purpose.
- Long-Range Goals and Vision.
- Mileposts for the Next One to Five Years.
- Next Actions by Priority.

Begin at the Beginning

You should always lead with your purpose statement and long-range goals based upon your vision. (You worked on this in Chapter 9). Sometimes we find that folks want to jump directly to what to do: mileposts and next actions, which is functionally tactical. Your experience creating and managing strategic plans tells you that beginning with the tactical never works. So now it's about you, so what should you do? Pull yourself up to 30,000 feet and begin with purpose and vision. Be strategic!

Purpose Is the Destination

In our changing world your purpose may be the one of the few things that won't need to be adapted over time. We find that even over relatively short periods of time (say, five years), your purpose is often the only thing that has not been tweaked to adapt to life's realities. Remember that our goal is for this document to function as a GPS rather than a static map. We want you to be able to adapt quickly and thoughtfully to whatever's on your road ahead. A well-thought-out purpose always represents the destination; it's how to get there that is the moving target.

If you haven't yet created your purpose statement, head back to Chapter 9. But if you've been working on it and you're still chewing and think perhaps you haven't got it just right yet, go ahead and put whatever your current draft is in your document. Just note that it is a draft. Sometimes going through the iterations of pulling this document together yields clarity about your purpose. So keep moving.

What's Nonnegotiable?

Your next exercise is to sketch out your long-range goals. When we asked you to put together a vision, you may have written a letter to a friend or a hypothetical schedule for a perfect day. Long-range goals should reflect very specifically your unique vision for your future. Don't be surprised if some of your long-range goals look like apple pie and motherhood. That's okay. For most of us these long-range goals include things for the long haul that just are not negotiable. It may help if we give you some examples.

We almost always see something about physical health and financial security:

- Stay healthy and active for as long as possible.
- Maintain financial security throughout my (our) lifetime(s).

It is hard to argue with these two, although you might phrase them differently.

And for those with kids we also see a variety of ways to say:

- See our children launched on their own lives of meaning.
- Assist our children in achieving financial sustainability on their own.

So this is your own life here. What about your vision for you? What other things might you include in your goals for the long term? The possibilities are unlimited for ideas. Look to your purpose statement, the visioning exercises, and the questions about finding your passions. Are you craving to give back in some way? Is there a second career in your future? Are you still figuring it all out? Well, get it down so you can make it happen. Here are some more examples:

- Travel outside the country for as long as I am able.
- Find an opportunity to teach children to fish.
- Interview my parents about the hardships they endured to create a memoir for future generations.
- Work in my profession as long as I am useful and not getting in anyone's way.
- Learn to speak a new language.
- Find a buyer for my business that will care about the customer as much as I do.

It's okay if some of this is still not as concrete as you would like, for example:

- Find an opportunity to start a new business in a completely new field.
- Experiment with volunteering in the business community.

- Consider joining a corporate board.
- Help children and pets.

The beauty of the plan we are asking you to create and execute is that it is designed with change in mind; in fact, change is expected. As you learn things, as you find clearer direction about what you'd like to do, the plan will naturally grow along with you.

What's Just Ahead?

These long-term goals are to be paired with short-term objectives. What kinds of things need to be accomplished in the near term to move the ball forward? In business strategy, this would be like an annual plan. Here we suggest a slightly longer time horizon—perhaps up to five years— recognizing that some human endeavors just take a bit more time. And we all know how quickly time seems to pass.

We call these *mileposts*. And as short-term objectives they should be just that—objective. You want to make your mileposts as concrete as you can so that it is possible to know whether or not you have passed them, let alone taken a detour around them.

In drafting mileposts, take a first look at the long-term goals. What specific thing needs to be done in the relatively near term to achieve each goal? It's also helpful to review your human capital balance sheet at this point. It can often reveal areas that you're ready to move on.

Some examples might include specifics of creating a healthier lifestyle (learning to cook) or finally getting some structures in place regarding your family's estate plan (create an education trust for your grandchildren). Or maybe it's time to figure out if the many checks you are writing to charities reflect what you really care about (assess charitable giving in light of your purpose). These are all items that take time and multiple steps to accomplish. But once they're done, the peace of mind is tremendous.

Then, Get Going

Finally, the plan needs to include the action steps needed to move along the way toward your mileposts. You say you want to get into better shape for golf? What is your next action? You want to consider downsizing the house? What is your next step? You want to reengage with your professional association? What's the next logical thing to do to move that forward?

Or perhaps you are still struggling with purpose and want to go away and think for a month or a year. What will you need to do to make that happen?

All of these things begin with the first step. Action steps are the most valuable when they clearly reflect what you should do next. This is how you hold yourself accountable. As you review what you've written, here is the test: Does this tell me clearly what to do? If not, keep at it until it does.

Sometimes it can be hard to tell the difference among long-range goals, mileposts, and action steps. Table 10.1 gives you an example of how that works best.

TABLE 10.1   Goals, Mileposts, and Steps for Action

Long-Range Goal	Stay healthy and active for as long as possible.
Milepost	Maintain a workout schedule that I enjoy.
Action Step	Find a group to walk with two to three days per week.

What to Do If You Still Don't Know What to Do

It is at this point that you want to return to the gnarliest of all questions, "If I am not working, what in the heck will I do all day long?" "Who will I be?" "Will anyone care what I think?"

While more time for leisure has some appeal, you still recognize a need for doing things that matter. There are a number of ways that individuals tackle this. You can use this as an idea generator for your plan:

1. Develop a pastime into an avocation. Is there something you already enjoy that you'd like to get really, really good at?
2. Find your inner artist. Is there some kind of creative pursuit that you'd like to try? Or some art or craft you did as a young person that got lost in life's shuffle?
3. Don't quit—morph. Can you stay with the same employer or industry and do something entirely new? Can you find more challenges?
4. Become a "learn-o-phile." Why not go back to school for the sheer joy of learning new things?

5. Teach—if a full-time regular classroom is too daunting, try volunteering.
6. Provide elder statesmanship. There is a need in industry, nonprofits, and government for those with gravitas and wisdom.
7. Become the thing you always wanted to be but couldn't as a younger person. Well, maybe firefighter or ballerina are now out of the question, but mayor or actress are probably still options. What was your dream?
8. Get your head clear so that you can sort it out. Interim steps can be:
   a. Nomadism—road trips, walkabouts.
   b. Change of venue—just move somewhere else for a while.
   c. Journaling.

Recognize that these things take time. Many of those that we talked to spent six months to two years before what to do became clear. So give yourself time. And as a last resort, we recommend pure, unbridled experimentation. Try some things and see what sticks. You might be shocked.

Finally, Let's Talk about Money

We suggested in Chapter 7 that you take a basic "first look" at what your financial future may hold. This is accomplished through the vehicle of the sustainability analysis; a personal financial forecast put together to give you a baseline about what the future might look like (there is a discussion of this in Appendix 2). This first pass was performed with some simplified assumptions to get in front of your headlights the most significant financial issues. For example, perhaps it helped you recognize that you cannot yet retire or that you have achieved the other end of the spectrum, you have more than you need. Both are important pieces of information.

You should know by now where you are on the wealth continuum shown in Figure 10.1.

Now it's time to refine this analysis. As you look over the draft of your Wealth Regeneration plan, you will undoubtedly see things that have financial impact. Those can now be incorporated into the sustainability analysis to test their viability.

Think of this as being much like scenario planning in a business setting. You can look at the alternative scenarios and make more informed decisions. This also positions you to respond to the unexpected. Once you have a solid grasp on sustainability, your ability to "recalculate route" is securely on your dashboard. All you have to do is pull together the new information and take a fresh look.

FIGURE 10.1 The Wealth Continuum

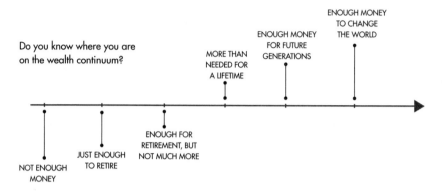

Focus on the scenarios that represent major financial implications, for example:

- Retiring today versus retiring in five years.
- Building a second home.
- Making a major philanthropic gift.
- Taking a year off.

And things like that. Looking at these big decisions yields highly instructive results.

Just don't get carried away with too many scenarios with small differences. The reality is, these types of tools, no matter how advanced they are, are blunt instruments. The findings should be thought of as directional in nature. You'll be able to judge from the results whether a $100,000 charitable gift is doable, but not whether a $95,000 or $105,000 gift would be better.

Also—and we'll talk about this more in the chapters ahead—don't rerun the scenarios too frequently. If you do, they begin to lose some of their effectiveness. You should actually pick one scenario as the baseline and stick to it for 12 to 18 months absent any game changers. More about that as we go on.

What If the Scenarios Suggest I'm Spending Too Much Money?

This can be a tough pill to swallow, but it is clearly better to know it sooner rather than later. It is not that unusual for successful people to allow their lifestyle costs to rise to the level of their cash flow. On top of that, business leaders often have perks embedded in their current package that will cost them real dollars once they move on. You have a company car? Is your golf club membership paid for? What about health insurance? All of these things must be considered in creating a scenario that delivers your sustainable future.

If the inescapable conclusion is that you must—or just want to—cut spending, check out Appendix 3. It lays out an alternative to traditional budgeting that has worked for many of our clients over the years. Even if you are not concerned about the spending levels, you might find that the system provides you with an elegant way to partner with your financial advisor in managing personal cash flows once you're no longer working.

A Word about Investment Policy

You need one, period, end of story. And this is the right time in your planning process to either assess the one you have or figure out how to get one. A good investment policy contains essentially the same elements as your Wealth Regeneration plan:

- Purpose.
- Long-range goals.
- Mileposts.
- Accountability.

Look familiar? A well-crafted investment policy supports your overall plan and becomes a focal point for decision making. It is also crucial to holding your investment people properly accountable. Your investment policy should not change much over time unless there are major changes in your life circumstances. Think of that policy statement as a foundational document and work with it accordingly.

You Can Do This

There's a lot to absorb here. The goal remains crafting a plan you will actually carry out. You want results, and that means execution. You want to stay on course, and that takes feedback. You have successfully executed on strategy in the past, so rely on what you know how to do. Again, at the end of the day, your plan is more likely to be accomplished if it incorporates those three principles: keeping it simple, making it actionable, and assigning clear accountability. Because that's what works.

PROFILE: JULIE WESTON AND GERRY MORRISON

Julie Weston and Gerry Morrison have been spouses and partners in life for over 30 years. Both had serious careers in the legal profession. Julie was the corporate secretary and general counsel for a substantial family-owned company. Gerry was a partner in what was at the time one of the largest law firms in Seattle, and served as the chair of that firm's business and transactions group. Clearly these are two people for whom career matters.

So when it came time to consider what was next, the stakes were high. Gerry began seriously contemplating retirement in his mid-50s. He had developed arthritis problems in his 40s. And things in the practice of law were changing in ways he was not comfortable with: "Now it felt like being a lawyer was more about CYA than giving the client practical advice." So at age 57 he retired.

A few years earlier, Julie had experienced burnout in corporate life. So she already had made a change, moving to doing freelance legal work and arbitrations rather than being someone else's employee.

In 1996, right before Gerry actually retired in 1997, they chose to spend an entire winter in Sun Valley. Both lifelong skiers, they looked at each other and said, "We can do this." And they did, beginning construction on a home in Idaho.

Still, they were clear that leisure, even spent doing something they loved as much as skiing, would never suffice; they naturally gravitated to finding something "real" to do.

As they describe their first year, it is as a time of being truly at loose ends. "It felt funny not to be doing the things we had always done." They had put together a detailed financial plan that addressed all the left-brain things in fine analytical form. What they found missing was the right brain. They realized they each had to find some compelling and creative activity.

Gerry reached back to a love of photography kindled in a high school darkroom in 1953. Since that time he has always had a darkroom in his home but, while working, rarely the time to use it. Now he had the time. Upon retirement he acquired the sort of large-format camera that Ansel Adams had used. With this classic kind of camera, you must view images upside down and inverted as you use it. As Gerry says dryly, "You learn how to really see things."

He became rapidly enmeshed in the art of photography and the different kind of intellectual discipline it represented. "I really enjoyed it—it was creative, fun, different—and clearly not the law." He further explains, "I would occasionally get calls from former clients wanting me to consult. But it just didn't work; my brain didn't work that way anymore." It seemed that once he turned to thinking artistically, he was hooked and could not go back.

Julie took a slightly longer path. She had begun writing in 1989, joining an avid writers group that met weekly for 10 years. As she puts it, "Writing is natural for lawyers. Lawyers have to write all the time." She found herself gradually working less and less and writing more and more—until the transformation was complete. For her, writing is what's called a flow activity, something in which she loses all track of time.

Today Julie and Gerry do both sit on corporate boards, but other than that their creativity is the central activity in their lives. Julie's memoir, *The Good Times Are All Gone Now* (published by the University of Oklahoma Press), is just nearing its fourth printing. She has had numerous short stories and essays published. There is also a novel or two in the works. Gerry has moved on from the darkroom to all digital but is still practicing his art as often as he can. Julie and Gerry have also collaborated, Julie writing an article about skiing for *Idaho Magazine* called "The Perfect Day," with Gerry providing the pictures.

As Julie and Gerry look back to what led them to where they are today, they credit a willingness to set the right sides of their brains free. As Julie points out, "We have always been active readers and that gets us thinking about lots of different things." Gerry says, "I actually think learning how to be artistic, working differently than I have ever worked before, may be the secret to a successful transition. It certainly was for me."

What will you create?

Toolkit

We have included here an example of the worksheet you will need to implement in this chapter.

Worksheet 1: Drafting Your Wealth Regeneration Plan

I. Purpose:

_____

_____

_____

_____

_____

(See Chapter 9 for reference.)

II. Long-range goals based upon vision:
   1. _____
     _____
     _____

   2. _____
     _____
     _____

   3. _____
     _____
     _____

   4. _____
     _____
     _____

   5. _____
     _____
     _____

   6. _____
     _____
     _____

What is life going to look like? You can have up to five long-range goals; more than that is difficult to plan for. Be sure to ask yourself if these goals reflect all aspects of your wealth. See Chapter 9 for details on developing your vision.

III. Mileposts for the next 1–5 years:
   1. _____
   2. _____
   3. _____
   4. _____
   5. _____

How do you know you are getting there from here?

IV. Next actions by priority:

TOP

Action	By When?	Who Owns?
1. _____	_____	_____
2. _____	_____	_____
3. _____	_____	_____
4. _____	_____	_____
5. _____	_____	_____

SHOULD DO

Action	By When?	Who Owns?
1. _____	_____	_____
2. _____	_____	_____
3. _____	_____	_____
4. _____	_____	_____
5. _____	_____	_____

WOULD BE NICE

Action	By When?	Who Owns?
1. _____	_____	_____
2. _____	_____	_____
3. _____	_____	_____
4. _____	_____	_____
5. _____	_____	_____

CHAPTER 11

Rolling It Forward

The final and most critical part of this or any plan remains what you do with it. We've already agreed that if you just stick it in a drawer or leave it in some dusty corner of your hard drive, it won't make much of a difference. That is so often the fate of the best-laid plans. Rather, you want to use this plan as a living, breathing guidance system—your personal GPS—and that means paying attention to it.

You remember the wheel, the process by which humans deal with change? This is essentially putting the concept of the wheel into action. If you haven't already noticed, your plan contains all the essential elements of the wheel, with one exception, rolling it forward. As we know, your wheel will only roll forward when somehow you discover that what you've been doing either never worked or isn't working any more and it's time to change it. It takes scrutiny to figure this out.

As you may recall from Chapter 6, every wheel needs a push in order to turn (see Figure 11.1).

We'd like to share with you how we've seen others use their plans effectively to find the push they need to get results over time.

Have a System

Ideally, you'll sit down with your plan and any related financial information on a periodic basis with the goal of giving yourself a check-in, a form of review, a chance to remind yourself about what's important and what you hope to achieve. This is most efficient and effective when it's done on a systematic basis. Let us describe to you an orderly way to do this that utilizes and leverages both your own skills and your key advisers. We have been

FIGURE 11.1 Pushing the Wheel

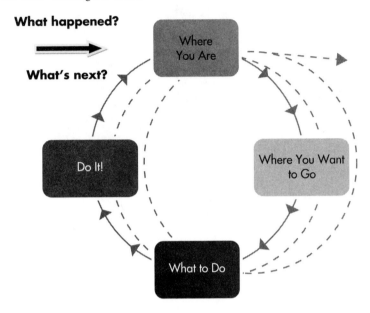

using variations on this approach with clients for years, so we can say with confidence that this type of check-in makes a difference.

There are really three kinds of check-ins you will need:

- The quick look: a high-level overview that you do every month or so, taking 30 minutes or less.
- The sit-down: a more intensive check-in, every three to six months, that gives you a reality check and reminds you to ask some hard questions, requiring 60 to 90 minutes. It should include a meeting or a call with your wealth manager.
- The deep dive: a top to bottom strategic look at your plan and its results, usually done every 12 to 18 months; this can take three or four hours.

If you keep to a consistent approach with each one of these check-ins, you'll achieve high level of oversight without too much time spent.

Once you have this cycle under your belt, we suggest one additional type of check-in—the all hands meeting. The all hands is another kind of deep dive. For this meeting, every member of your team comes together. This includes your wealth manager, your CPA, and your attorney, all together in one room (and of course that room can be virtual). The goal is to make sure that everyone has the latest view of your thoughts and objectives as well as your financial situation, so that all the best ideas are on the table.

We propose that for all three kinds of check-ins you look at both human capital and financial capital. Most people only look at the financial capital, opening the statements as they come in, calling or meeting with their financial advisor. You will take a more global and proactive look that includes all aspects of your wealth.

The Quick Look Check-In

The first kind of check-in should happen every month or two. We will call it a quick look because that is exactly what it should be. In business you usually have a dashboard of key factors that you frequently monitor to get results. The goal is engineering the same thing for your wealth.

Begin by simply reading your plan and reminding yourself what you said. (Remember, the plan is short, maybe two pages max.) Does it still ring true? Are you fulfilling the promises you made yourself? Are you actually taking action on the action steps you committed to? Rereading the plan keeps you in touch with the human capital aspects of your wealth.

Now, on to the financial. And how are your investments doing? It's nice to have a way to look at financial data that is simple and consistent. Since most of the paperwork you receive is voluminous, it helps to identify the top two or three factors that you will look at religiously, time after time. Consider asking your advisor to walk you through your statements and performance reports with an eye to what you should be looking at most frequently. Again be thinking dashboard, not looking at every single page of 30 pages of account statements.

The Sit-Down

You'll want to do a more detailed check-in every six months or so. Again, get your plan document in front of you and review it. Make specific notes of what's working and what's not. Were some of your next actions unrealistic? Do you need to find a way to nudge yourself here or there to get things done? Does someone else need a push? Do you need to just hire someone to make it happen? At this check-in it's all about making sure that the next actions get done.

Pair this with a more detailed conversation with your advisor. Are you still on track financially? Have you been affected materially by any economic or market conditions? Ordinary market volatility is generally not a sign of any need to change. This is more about tactical opportunity. For both of the shorter check-ins we strongly recommend that you make and keep notes on your observations. Doesn't mean you change anything in the plan, but it does give you additional insight when it's time for the deep dive.

Now for the Deep Dive

Every year to 18 months it is time for the full meal deal. Pull out the document and do a thorough written assessment with an eye to creating a new version. This is actually less complicated than it sounds. There's no need to write any kind of narrative. You're not going to start from scratch, either; think of this as more like version 2.0. You simply go through the document along with the notes you've been keeping and determine what can roll forward and what might need changing. Figure 11.2 shows our flowchart.

FIGURE 11.2   Flowcharting What Happened

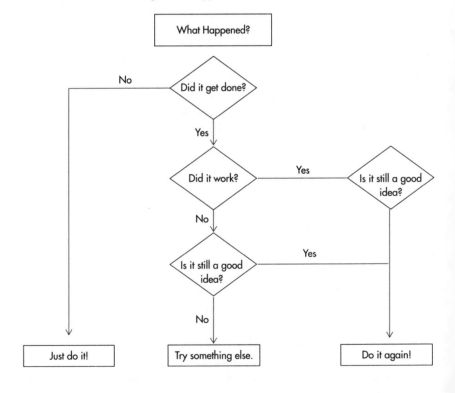

It also makes sense to do an update of your two balance sheets at this point—both financial and human capital. Where are these today? And how do they compare with where you started?

At the time of the deep dive, your sustainability analysis also should be scrubbed. Ask your advisor for a list of all the original assumptions over which you have control—like what you spend or what you earn. Review them with an eye for changes. Remember that cash flows in and out are key drivers. Is your spending on track? Are you considering a big charitable pledge? Has someone made you an offer you can't refuse for your business?

Further, you want to review the embedded assumptions that your advisor is making about markets and the economy. Has he or she made any changes to their view of what the future looks like? Are you comfortable with either their pessimism or optimism?

Once this is done, be sure that the analysis is actually rerun. There may be no changes other than your age and investment balances. That's okay. It should be rerun anyway. Even modest changes in any category or assumption may have an effect. You want to see that, even if it doesn't change what you're planning to do.

Don't forget the sustainability analysis is just an estimation process. Every 12 to 18 months is the right interval to have it run. More frequently adds no value and may actually be confusing.

At this point you should also look at your investment policy. It is not likely to change, but you want to reconfirm that its parameters remain appropriate to your plan.

Table 11.1 gives you a summary of the recommended check-ins.

TABLE 11.1 Summary of Check-ins

	Frequency	Human Capital	Financial Capital
The Quick Look	Every 30–60 days	Reread plan, note progress and challenges.	Look at investment dashboard.
The Sit-Down	Every 3–6 months	Reread plan, note progress and challenges, revamp next actions as needed.	Get detailed update from investment advisor, including performance review.
The Deep Dive	Every 12–18 months	Review plan in detail. Update Human Capital Balance Sheet. Make changes to plan as needed.	Update Financial Balance Sheet. Update Sustainability Analysis. Reconfirm Investment Policy.

Finally, prepare to roll your plan forward. This is the tipping point of the Wealth Regeneration wheel. Will you keep doing the same things over and over (remember, that is perfectly okay if you are getting the desired outcome)? Or is it time for a change? Let's roll 'em!

Keeping the Plan

Like most goal-oriented people, we like to see plans maintained and updated in a way that lets us look back at history. This is not merely to be self-congratulatory or self-flagellating. Presenting data from multiple periods side-by-side makes it much easier to spot patterns. Remember, you're asking questions like "What happened?" "Did it work?" "Did I get what I wanted?" In a perfect world you would like your existing plans side-by-side with any proposed update, in the same format. And once you commit to the update—accept it as your new plan—you should still be able to look back at your trajectory. On the financial capital side it is pretty easy (see Table 11.2).

On the human side, we suggest you keep copies of the human capital balance sheet from period to period with your detailed notes. Basically we are saying hit the "save as," rather than the "save" when you are updating your document. Some people take the old-school route of keeping a binder. Others may use an Excel spreadsheet setting plans side-by-side. (Kaycee prefers binders, Bob is strongly in favor of the electronic solution.) However you prefer to do it is fine as long as you *do* do it.

We can't emphasize enough the importance of this regular deep dive. There are times to stay with the status quo, and there are times to move on. How often in your life have you said "I wish I had done that sooner"? The goal of the deep dive is to find those things sooner so we can adapt sooner—or confirm that we don't see any change at all. There is nothing wrong with the decision to make no changes, just as long it as it is a decision rather than acquiescence. This is precisely what the concept of the wheel is all about.

TABLE 11.2 Looking at History

	Two Years Ago	Last Year	This Year
Net Worth			
Annual Spending			

Where the Rubber Most Likely Meets the Road

More often than not you'll find that some portions of your document have truly stood up to the passage of time. Other pieces, not so much. Our experience suggests that where you will have the most assessment to do is in the next actions area. At the very least one might hope a few of those next actions have been completed. As you review the items, if you see things that just never happened, ask yourself these questions:

Why not?

• Never got around to it?
• No longer relevant?
• I'm uncomfortable doing it?

Does it still really need to be done? Or are you setting yourself up? If so, what will break it loose?

• Hire someone else to do it?
• Find another way to do it?
• Get someone to shepherd you through it?

This gives you a pretty clear-eyed look at it the gap between what you said you would do and what you actually have done. It also sets the stage for you to ask yourself what new items should be considered. Are there new items for action? We hope so; that keeps your plan fresh. Clearly, this kind of review requires effort, but it also drives results.

The Big Picture

As you know our Wealth Regeneration mantra is:

• Tend your financial capital very, very well.
• Mind your human capital with at least as much fervor as you give your financial capital.
• Stay open to adaptation in the face of change.

These tenets have stood the test of time, generation after generation. Your plan should serve you just as well. This review process is designed to get you going on all cylinders. You look at financial capital, you look at human capital, and you identify opportunities for adaptation. You keep rolling forward. That is Wealth Regeneration in action.

When Stuff Happens

As you might expect, there is another point where the full meal deal intensive review needs to be done. And that's when your life changes in such a way that the bulk of the assumptions in your plan may no longer be relevant. These times can include the self-selected:

- "I'm just tired. I want to retire this year, not in five years."
- "I have really wrapped my head around my purpose and the right thing for me to do is go run that nonprofit that I have been volunteering for."

These are big changes.

Yet sometimes even bigger are the events that life just tosses at you. Perhaps it is divorce, or death, or a health crisis. In every case the same methodology of the deep dive still applies. You can just slip right into the routine.

We can say from experience that in times of crisis there is nothing more comforting than the familiar. Even if everything else is up in the air, you at least know what to do when it comes to this area of your life. You can get on with "recalculate route." Your Wealth Regeneration GPS is at your service.

There will still be difficult questions to be answered, but the process is never in doubt (see Figure 11.3).

As an added benefit, we can tell you that the forward motion of the Wealth Regeneration wheel creates a kind of gyroscope effect. Somehow,

FIGURE 11.3 The Wheel Keeps Turning

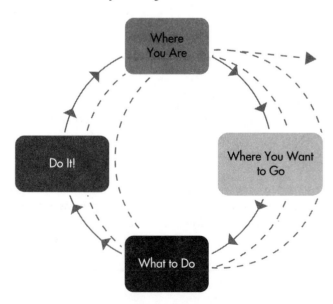

when you think things may just topple over, the movement of the wheel pulls you upright. You just keep rolling along.

What to Share with Your Advisor

As we have gone through this process, we noted areas where we believe it is essential to work closely with your financial advisor. But we recommend you go further than these essentials. You'll find the more they know, the better positioned your trusted advisor will be to give you the advice you need. So consider sharing all of this process and the results. You won't be wasting their time or yours. Understanding the things that matter most to you positions your advisor to be the thought partner you need along the way.

The Time Is Now

The processes we have outlined here are fairly simple and are purposely designed for time efficiency. They are also designed to help you pull up to the strategic level from time to time, so that what the plan is all about remains central. Remember that Wealth Regeneration is fundamentally strategic planning for your life, so it just makes sense to take the time to be sure to execute.

PROFILE: STEVE ALTMAYER

Steve Altmayer finally retired three years after selling his business, Wrap Pak, to a private equity firm. He found himself in the unique and enviable position of having sold to good partners. So he enjoyed continuing to work. After the first three years he helped them sell it again, finally moving on to real retirement.

Steve grew up in Florida with very modest means. A careful observer of people and how they lived, he determined he wanted to be an airline pilot. From his vantage point they (a) always seemed to have money, (b) always seemed to have the best toys (boats and cars), and (c) didn't seem to work all that much. What teenage boy didn't want to grab that ring?

In pursuing this goal he joined Navy ROTC, which took him to Wharton for his undergraduate degree. His intention was to be trained as a pilot in the Navy and thereby go straight into the glidepath for his chosen career. But such was not to be. Steve made it into flight school all right, but discovered that he simply hated to fly.

After the Navy, one of his fellow students at Wharton convinced him to consider working for his family-owned paper company. Once there

(continued)

Steve did well and rose quickly. He became the CFO and ultimately was chosen to run a subsidiary that later became Wrap Pak. While you may never have heard of Wrap Pak, if you have ever eaten a pear, you have certainly used its products. About 80 percent of the pears in the United States arrived wrapped in special papers from Wrap Pak. Steve was able to purchase Wrap Pak from his employer and grew it successfully for over 10 years. Then one day he realized he had not only achieved the financial success he had hoped would be possible by working for the airlines—he had exceeded it. It was time to move on. So he initiated a sales process.

Once the final transaction was complete, in analyzing his next moves, Steve referred to Maslow's hierarchy of needs. "I had now achieved all the basics—I can focus on the top of the pyramid. What did self-actualization mean to me?"

He identified four areas to focus on—health and wellness, spirituality, self-expression and creativity, and intellectual development. In short, Steve was about to become very much a Renaissance man.

He began on the self-expression and creativity front by spending two years in culinary school, ultimately working as a sous chef in a Michelin-starred restaurant in France. For health and wellness he took up running for the first time in his life and has now completed a half marathon. "That's about as far as I want to run," he says. His current intellectual targets are physics and Buddhism.

Meanwhile Steve stayed active in Rotary and the nonprofit called Smile Train, which arranges for children in developing countries to have surgeries to correct a cleft palate. He and his wife live in France several months of the year, although he so far has avoided learning to speak the language. Apparently that has not yet come up on his radar screen as desired intellectual development.

Steve has wise words for others who are moving on. First, he says, "Make sure you understand what you are giving up." If you have been "somebody" throughout your career, maybe you need to find a way to still be "somebody" in your next phase. He also notes, "And be careful what you say, you may just have to do it." Steve had told so many people that he wanted to go to culinary school that as soon as his retirement became fact, he was besieged by those wanting to know when he was going. So he went. He says now he might've prioritized things differently.

At the end of the day, Steve has built a very engaging life for himself, one that encompasses growth and learning along with challenges and the satisfaction of giving back. Steve seized the opportunity of retirement to be "somebody"—and that somebody is himself.

Who will you be?

CHAPTER 12

Legacy

What is legacy, anyway? The word certainly gets used a lot. Most of us think of it as a name on a building or endowment. But it is both more profound and more subtle than that.

The trap that many successful people fall into is believing that legacy is about money. It's not—it's about action and about how you live your life every day. In fact, the great paradox is that you cannot leave a legacy unless you live it first. What are the things you are doing each day that reflect who you are and your real purpose in life? That's where legacy comes from.

We boomers are entering that stage of life when attending memorial services is more commonplace. Have you been to one where you walked out thinking "Wow, this guy (or gal) really made a difference"? Maybe it was because the hall was packed with people. Or maybe it was because those readings and speeches were so heartfelt. Or perhaps it was how, after it was all over, people stood around in groups to swap stories of all the differences the deceased had made, both large and small. So here's today's tough question—would anyone show up for your service? Or do you even care?

Not all of us are seeking to be memorialized (Kaycee wants a huge party, Bob is thankfully more dignified) but most of us would like to think we have had some lasting impact.

You already have a legacy, whether intentional or not. Based upon your actions today, people either will or will not remember you. Their lives will or will not be better because you existed. That's legacy.

The reality is that even if someone walks into a beautiful new building with your name on it, they may not experience your legacy. Real legacy exists when someone's life is clearly different because you were there.

It does not have to be a huge thing to create real treasure for future generations. Working side-by-side with your grandchildren in the garden gives them the gift of a sense of personal accomplishment. Or letting them ride along shotgun as you volunteer to help others gives them a window into how other people live. These are clearly legacy builders. You may be doing things like this in the community or in your business life as well. But are you doing enough? And are you being intentional about the impacts created?

That impact could be as simple as a grandchild whose eyes are opened to the world on a special trip with grandparents. Or a young business owner, struggling to make a go, now guided by a seasoned mentor. The list of possibilities is endless. It is the sum total of these things that creates a real legacy.

What we'd like to suggest here is that you crank it up a notch. The work you've been doing so far to plan for your life and for your wealth translates beautifully into creating an intentional legacy. And this is clearly a task best done on purpose.

If you take a look at your purpose and plan, you will undoubtedly find the essential ingredients of legacy already there. The question to ask yourself is, How should I prioritize them? Interestingly, legacy-producing activities often get pushed to the back burner as the imperatives of day-to-day living take center stage.

When was the last time you mentored someone? Shoot, you have been meaning to schedule that trip with the grandkids, why haven't you done it? Gosh, you keep missing the meetings of that nonprofit board you are on—are you really committed to them? These are some of the questions you'll wrestle with.

There Are Challenges

Often when you begin to address these issues you get funneled directly onto a side road labeled estate planning. We have all done it—gotten so caught up in who will be the executor or how much tax we want to avoid that we have lost sight of the purpose of the exercise. At the end of the day (and this time it really *is* about the end of the day), are those things you care the most about?

It's not that saving taxes or avoiding probate are not valid outcomes. The big question is: Are they right for you and your family? Are they your highest priorities? Do they further your purpose? Will they make any kind of difference in people's lives after you're gone?

Even the most skilled estate planners fall into these traps. Take a look at the diagram in Figure 12.1.

FIGURE 12.1 Why Is This So Difficult?

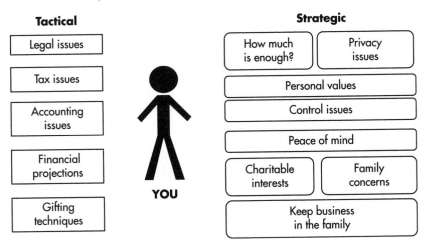

Tactical

Legal issues

Tax issues

Accounting issues

Financial projections

Gifting techniques

YOU

Strategic

How much is enough?

Privacy issues

Personal values

Control issues

Peace of mind

Charitable interests

Family concerns

Keep business in the family

Source: Adapted from Richard and Linda Livingston, *Smart and Caring (RDL Publishing, 1999).*

What almost always happens is that you inadvertently get so caught up in the tactical side of the diagram that you don't fully attend to the *why* of it all. Plus, it's always easier to talk about saving taxes than what kind of inheritance is right for your children. That's why we propose that you create a guide for your estate planners and family that sets everyone on the right course, yourself included.

We call this guide a *letter of intent.* It is loosely based upon the Judaic tradition of an ethical will. In this letter you lay out as specifically as you can what matters most to you and why. This letter becomes the starting place and the cornerstone for all the rest of the planning for your estate. The result is a much more personal planning process with less wasted effort. You'll avoid exploring options that may not be a good fit and quite possibly even experience lower legal fees.

Of course, we are sure this is not you we are talking about here . . . but it is incredibly common that estate plans are drafted and then languish in home office desk drawers unsigned. More often than not we find this occurs because the documents are all about the left side of that diagram, and they don't address your true key concerns. With the best of intentions, the professionals trying to help you come to the party with their own headsets. If they have not gotten super-clear guidance from you, they do their darnedest to get the job done based upon their unique experience. And that can lead to places that might not be the right fit for you. Something just doesn't feel right, so you never get around to signing the documents.

A letter of intent is a way for you to get out in front of this. Creating one is actually pretty simple once you have a Wealth Regeneration discipline in place. You've already done the work; it's just a matter of taking it a step further.

What a Letter of Intent Looks Like

We like to see a letter of intent set up as a fairly straightforward document. Here is an outline of a letter of intent with some explanations of each section.

Outline of Letter of Intent

- Purpose
- History
- What I/we think is important
- Responsibility to myself/ourselves
- Responsibility to my/our heirs
- Responsibility to my/our extended family
- Responsibility to the community
- Structural considerations
- Taxes
- Next steps

1. Purpose of the Letter—Here you explain who this letter is for and why you have written it. Occasionally the only audience is your professional advisors. We do recommend that the scope be expanded to include your heirs. It can be a wonderful way for family to understand why things are the way they are.

2. History—Here you lay out both financial history and personal history. If you have received an inheritance, your experience as an inheritor may also be instructive. Did you struggle to achieve success? Have you experienced privation? Particularly for those in blended families, the financial history can be very important. You'll be surprised how often family members are in the dark about where wealth came from. Do you have separate property or joint property? Did you ever live in a community property state?

3. What We Think Is Important—This is an opportunity to articulate your values. We suggest that you be as concrete as possible so there is less

opportunity for misinterpretation. This is the place to expand on how you define fairness. It's our experience that every heir has his or her own definition of what's "fair." But as the person doing the planning, it is really up to you to set the ground rules.

4. Responsibilities—In this section you lay out how you see your responsibilities to various stakeholders. We suggest you break it out as responsibility to:

- Ourselves.
- Our heirs.
- Our extended family.
- And the community.

You'll note that we indicate that your first responsibility is to yourself. This is not by accident; in fact, we found that this can be a key to leveraging your estate plan. You intend to live life to the fullest and whatever's left over is whatever is left over? Or will you make sacrifices to be able to benefit other stakeholders? Realistically, this is something of a continuum and everyone needs to know where you stand. How do you see your responsibility to your heirs? For most people the primary heirs are children, but some of the same principles apply with all heirs. How much is enough? Do you want them to have a successful launch in life? To provide a safety net throughout their lifetimes for, say, health or other risks? To provide opportunities to pursue careers that may not be as financially rewarding but are driven by passion? There's a lot to think about here. Use this section to describe your hopes and dreams for each stakeholder.

5. Structural Considerations—We suggest that you include anything that you have preferences about, like privacy or control. Do you get very uncomfortable if you transfer control to others? How much do you want family members to know and when do you want them to know it? How comfortable are you at dealing with complexity? These can all affect your plan.

6. Taxes—Here again there is a continuum. Your team needs to know where you fit. Is avoiding taxes your highest priority? Or is it more important to achieve your personal objectives? The reality is that there are always trade-offs to be made. There are almost always ways to avoid tax but often the cost is diverting assets away from desired recipients. How will you make these choices?

7. Next Steps—This is a simple statement of intended actions springing from the prior items. It is not intended to lay out the plan; rather, it is intended to state what you, as the principal in your plan, intend to do next.

Here are some examples of the kinds of statements you might make in a letter of intent.

- Purpose: "We have written this letter to serve as a guide for professional advisors and family as we plan for the future. Our goal is to set down our ideas in the hopes that this will assist all of us in creating and executing the best possible plan."
- Responsibility to ourselves: "We expect to maintain our lifestyle as it is today throughout our lifetimes. In any long-range plan we want to be certain that the assets we need to sustain us are available to us."
- Responsibility to our heirs: "We want our children to have every opportunity to achieve their potential whether in business, teaching, philanthropy, or another positive pursuit."
- Responsibility to our extended family: "Our siblings have not been as financially fortunate as we have been. We would like to find a way to provide them with a safety net for the remainder of their lifetimes."
- Responsibility to the community: "We are very interested in helping improve public education. We would consider making larger gifts to that area of interest, particularly if it were possible to engage our children in the process."
- Structural considerations: "We have always been very private about our families' affairs, so we would like to avoid any tools or techniques that might cause our affairs to be made public."

As you can see, these are all things that can impact how you craft an estate plan. The sooner your estate planning team is aware of them, the better, and the clearer you make your communication, the better as well.

Seriously, This Isn't That Hard

You may be looking at this and saying, "This seems like an awful lot of effort; wow, writing a letter, well, maybe I'll get to that in a year or so." While we recommend a letter format (and we can tell you it has worked well for many, many clients over the years), it is not the only format. Quite frankly, if you just take this outline and jot down notes and bullet points and take them to your estate planning meetings with you, much will be accomplished. What you miss out on if you have no letter is having a document that the family can look at after you're gone that reveals the *why* of it all.

And whether you write the letter or not, please check out Worksheet 2, our list of things to decide *before* you get to your estate planner's office. It can be a big time saver.

If all else fails, in his book *Family Wealth—Keeping It in the Family*, Jay Hughes offers an engaging exercise that might get your juices flowing. Jay suggests this as part of a family meeting agenda but we find it works beautifully as a solo gig as well. In it he asks you to imagine that you are 105 years old (think Old Lodge Skins in "Little Big Man"). Now, what would you like to share with those around you? That's exactly what your family and your advisors need to know.

So let's go back to our opening discussion about legacy. It truly means taking action in ways that make a lasting difference in people's lives. Most of that activity needs to be part of your day-to-day life to have impact. But by crafting a letter of intent, you can make sure that what you leave behind tells the same story.

Legacy Is Generativity in Action

Throughout our lives, we have all known acquaintances and colleagues whose only modus operandi was "what's in it for me." Didn't you find yourself avoiding them whenever possible? Perhaps they achieved initial successes, but later flamed out in some way. Thankfully, as we all get older this behavior is usually outgrown. We move naturally from a focus on individual success to success as a team—from "me to we."

Later life brings us to a new stage—generativity. Generativity occurs when you begin to feel that you must do more, that you want to create success for others—success that goes beyond your own.

This is different from a desire for success as a team, and it is what motivates real legacy. To use an analogy, in the "me" phase you might row your boat alone across a wide river. In the "we" phase you are in a boat where all (hopefully) row together—or at least that is the intention. Once you reach generativity, you don't even get in the boat. Instead, you stand on the shore to give those boats a big shove off, and then cheer wildly as they reach the other side. You have moved from "me" to "we" to "them."

The impulse to generativity is what inspires the actions that lead to legacies. Whether purposefully done or not, it is those who have shoved off the most boats who are the longest remembered. And that's real legacy.

Have you shoved off any boats lately?

PROFILE: BETH BAZLEY

In 2003 at age 41, Paul Bazley retired from Microsoft. Paul was a nine-year veteran at Microsoft, a marketing manager who had attained the vice presidential level in the company. Like so many of his colleagues who also chose to retire early, he had loved his years at Microsoft, but now he was burned out and needed to refresh and reconnect with his family.

Paul and his wife Beth met while working at IBM as interns during college. Paul accepted a position with IBM in 1983 and went to Alaska. Beth followed him shortly thereafter, taking a position with Xerox.

Paul and Beth thrived in Alaska, both working for great companies while enjoying the beauty of the state. By the early 1990s they were starting their family, which gave Beth the opportunity, as she puts it, "to take a promotion to full-time mom." At the same time, Paul began to see things stagnating at IBM and he began to search for a new challenge.

That challenge came in the form of an opportunity with Microsoft in 1994. In those days Microsoft was not yet the behemoth that it would become. When Paul started there were only 5,000 people. The change in culture from IBM to Microsoft was dramatic and positive. Paul found the "go to it" attitude at Microsoft invigorating. He learned and progressed rapidly in an environment that showed him both his strengths and his limitations. He loved it.

Paul was by nature a planner, always taking careful care of the family's finances. As he began to recognize that he might need a change of pace, it was natural to think about planning. He and Beth, working together with their newly hired advisor, put an even more detailed plan together. This plan addressed both their financial capital (yes, you have enough money to retire) and their human capital (yes, you can travel with your daughters to see all seven continents before they graduate from high school). With the plan in place, Paul retired and promptly spent the next four months sleeping.

Paul and Beth jumped into this new situation with both feet. While what might be next for Paul professionally was not clear, other things were crystal clear. Paul and Beth's girls were at ages where they were thrilled to have more of their daddy in their lives. And Paul needed to learn how to take better care of himself.

As time progressed, Paul began to think more about his return to the work world. A good friend had introduced him to a consulting opportunity, and that was going very well. The family had taken their first two trips on their great inter-continental adventures having crossed the Canadian Rockies by train, toured the highlights of Europe, explored all over Australia, and visited South America, especially enjoying the Galapagos Islands and Peru. Visiting Machu Picchu had been a lifelong dream of Paul's. Life was pretty good.

One day Paul went out for a bike ride and did not come home. He suffered a massive heart failure and was probably dead before he hit the ground.

Beth says it clearly: "There are few times in life that are truly transformative; this was one of them. I needed to discover how to be the leader of our family."

The plan made all the difference. Not only were Paul and Beth's financial affairs already in good order, there was already a process and a team in place to move forward and begin to make the difficult decisions. Beth did not have to pull herself up the steepest part of the learning curve. She had help. Did it make dealing with this tragedy easier? Probably not that, but certainly less hard.

But the most poignant part of all this and the most important is the human capital aspect of the plan. "Take our girls to see all seven continents before they leave high school." Beth remained committed to the goal of having the girls see all seven continents before they left high school, raising her daughters to be citizens of the world in her shared vision with Paul.

Today all seven continents have been visited, and Beth and Paul's oldest child is in college. Beth is looking at her own "what's next" right now. She discovered a personal talent for fundraising and is hard at work in the independent school sector. There is a new plan in place for the family now.

When asked to describe her experience, Beth likens it to being on a bullet train: "You're heading out on a set of tracks at super high speed, then something happens. Will you just be derailed or can you jump to the next set of tracks? We were able to jump to the next set of tracks."

And that's why planning matters.

Will your plan survive you?

Toolkit

We have included examples of the worksheets and tools you will need to implement in this chapter:

1. Outline of Letter of Intent.
2. Things to Decide *before* You Get in Your Lawyer's Office.

Worksheet 1: Outline of Letter of Intent

Write some things down!

1. Purpose of the letter:
   Why am I writing this? Who is my audience?

   _____

   _____

   _____

   _____

   _____

   _____

2. History:
   What is my background? Where did the wealth come from?

   _____

   _____

   _____

   _____

   _____

   _____

3. What I/we think is important:
   What do I value?

   _____

   _____

   _____

   _____

   _____

   _____

4. Responsibility to myself/ourselves:

   _____

   _____

   _____

   _____

   _____

   _____

5. Responsibility to my/our heirs:

_____
_____
_____
_____
_____
_____

6. Responsibility to my/our extended family:

_____
_____
_____
_____
_____
_____

7. Responsibility to the community:

_____
_____
_____
_____
_____
_____

8. Structural considerations:
   What works and doesn't work for me? Privacy? Control? Complexity?

_____
_____
_____
_____
_____
_____

9. Taxes:
What priority level do I give to saving taxes? What am I willing to give up to save taxes?

_____

_____

_____

_____

_____

_____

_____

10. Next steps:

_____

_____

_____

_____

_____

_____

_____

Worksheet 2: Things to Decide *before* You Get in Your Lawyer's Office

1. If you die before your spouse, are you willing to leave your estate to your spouse with no strings attached?

_____

_____

_____

_____

_____

_____

2. If you both die, would you like to have your entire estate held as a common fund for your children, or would you like to have each of your children have his or her separate trust fund?

_____

_____

_____

_____

3. At what age (or ages) would your children be entitled to receive their inheritance outright, free and clear of any trust?

_____

_____

_____

_____

_____

_____

4. Who do you want to act as your personal representative or executor?

_____

_____

_____

5. Who do you want to serve as trustees of the trusts established for your children?

_____

_____

_____

6. Who would you like to serve as the guardian for your minor children if both of you die?

_____

_____

_____

7. If your entire family dies in a common disaster, whom should the estate pass to?

_____

_____

_____

8. What specific items of property would you like to leave to designated individuals?

_____

_____

_____

9. Do you want any portion of your estate passed to charity?

_____

_____

_____

And in Conclusion

As you reach the end of this road with us, there are several thoughts we'd like to leave with you.

You Are in Charge

All along the way we have acknowledged that to be our reader you are most likely successful—the kind of person who has risen to leadership. That means you also have a finely honed sense of what works for you and what does not. We encourage you to use that.

Some who prescribe a way of doing things, as we have here with Wealth Regeneration, demand that you follow their approach to the letter. Otherwise, they say, it won't work. Well, we are not that hubristic. We have learned over many years and many client situations that different techniques work for different people. The important thing is finding a technique that works best for *you*.

That's why we have presented so many tools and techniques here. Our desire is that you can easily find the things that will work for you. So if there are techniques or exercises we have suggested that don't feel quite right to you, pass on them. Go to what resonates; go to what your gut tells you will be most helpful.

The Bare Essentials

That being said, we would encourage you to be adventurous. Because we have so many years of client experience under our belts, we know there are a few things that work for almost everyone. In fact, these are the elements of the Wealth Regeneration toolkit that are most determinative of success or failure. So if you take nothing else away be sure to give these a try:

The Wheel Model—Understanding and embracing the model of change and progress that the wheel represents is foundational. You will find it works in many settings. However you do it, some function of accountability or assessment that allows you to spot when you are in a rut makes all the difference. That is not to say that the wheel does not occasionally roll backward. That is just life. But it is unlikely to roll forward with any consistency without the kind of careful thought that regular assessment and accountability bring to the table. Sometimes the wheel just needs a tiny push.

Purpose—Yes, here we go pushing that touchy-feely stuff again. A purpose statement or something like it is key. If you don't have some standard or goal to hold current conditions and choices up against, it is virtually impossible to make good decisions. Quite honestly, we don't care what you call it, but some concrete sense of what matters most provides great leverage when the chips are down. That purpose gives you the clarity to sort through competing alternatives. Whatever you call it, you've got to have one. And no, you don't have to tell anyone about it!

Write it down—Throughout this book we've given you ample opportunity to write, whether it's financial facts or your hopes and dreams. Whatever part of the Wealth Regeneration discipline you choose to employ, documenting what you've done and the decisions you've made—then keeping it somewhere where you can find it again—pays off. We've mentioned before the classic statement attributed to Peter Drucker, that "whatever gets measured, gets managed." Well here's our version when it comes to documentation: "Whatever gets documented, gets done." We agree it's not always true, but true enough often enough to make writing down (and that includes keyboarding) your intentions a powerful tool for success.

That Being Said . . .

Now, we have just told you that you don't *have* to use all the tools and techniques we've included here, and it's true up to a point. But we do want you to know, based upon meeting after meeting with high-powered people in the midst of change, just like you, that this process is unpredictable. You may have rules you've successfully followed through other changes in your life in the past that just don't seem to be operational here. Sometimes you don't know what works until you give it a try. And sometimes you try things that seem sure to be uncomfortable that end up surprising you.

Over the years we have used these techniques in many face-to-face client situations. We actually will sit in the same room with the client as they write or in some cases we ask the questions and write the answers down on the client's behalf. We may even draft the plans or letters of intent for them to edit. But no matter how we do it, we consistently see the same phenomenon. The client may begin the session fidgeting and checking his or her watch (well, nowadays, iPhone); yet the client ends the session thoroughly engaged in plotting the strategy for his or her own life and wealth. Because what could be more important?

Pulling Yourself Up to the Top of the Mountain

So if you're ready to get started, here are the tasks, organized by chapter. And not coincidentally, by the model of the wheel:

• Know where you are (and who you are).
• Know what you want (and where you want to go).
• Decide what to do (and how to get there from here)—
• Then rolling it forward.

And of course you get bonus points if you also work on embracing your legacy. Kidding (well, not really)!

We told you at the outset that this was not rocket science, and that you, with a track record of leadership, had all the skills you need to be successful. You'll have to admit we were right. If you lay it out this way it is not quite so daunting. And to make it even easier, just head to our website at www.LNTyee.com where you can download all the worksheets and tools in a PDF form. Piece of cake.

We hope you have enjoyed the stories that we've shared with you about others who've made the transition and found what's next. Not everyone will be a French chef or composer of music, but we all have something important left to do. Wealth Regeneration is all about helping you find it.

If you reach out to others and ask about their transitions, we expect you'll hear more amazing stories. Particularly if what's next for you is still murky, asking others to share what works for them helps put the spotlight on the road ahead. We've included the interview format that we used in gathering the profiles as Appendix 4. We hope you have found them instructive and inspirational. We heard many stories along the way. Take someone out for coffee and start asking these questions. There's always something to learn.

Both of us wish to thank you for the perseverance you have shown to come this far with us. We believe that helping successful people stay successful throughout their lifetimes is important work and makes a difference in the world. It lies closely aligned with our own life purposes. We are honored that you spent this time with us.

Every success to you.

Appendix 1: How to Choose a Wealth Advisor

Building teams is one of the core competencies you have as a leader. Now it's time to get started on building your own Wealth Regeneration team. Here you will seek a variety of skill sets: a strong estate planner, a skilled tax manager, someone to forecast the future, and an investment strategist will certainly be on the list. You may also find, depending upon your circumstances, that you want someone to pay bills, be a trustee, manage your airplane, or perform any of the myriad other tasks that are unique to you. This will be your team.

In most cases the team consists of an attorney, a CPA, and a wealth advisor. Since we suspect that you have had experience hiring attorneys and accountants before, we will focus here on the role of the wealth advisor and how to find one.

When you're hiring to fill the role of the wealth advisor, whether for the first time or making a change, you'll find that some complexities arise. You have dealt with CPAs and attorneys before, and for both those professions standards are fairly well understood. The field of wealth management, however, may be entirely new territory for you. As in any search, the quality of your decision is a direct reflection of the quality of the questions that you ask. So we have laid out our list of questions for you to ask your potential wealth advisor.

But first, how do you find one? This is tough because the term "wealth manager" or "financial advisor" is unregulated. Anyone, from stockbrokers to insurance agents, can hold him- or herself out as a wealth manager. What we want you to have on your team is someone who is a true advisor, not someone whose primary goal is to sell you something. Further, we want you to have an advisor who really understands the strategy piece of the planning process, not just someone with tactical ideas to throw at you. And finally, we want you to have someone with the level of sophistication you need to address the complexity of your life transition.

Often the best way to find these individuals is through good old-fashioned networking, only with a twist. Definitely ask your friends and people you respect in your community whom they use and would recommend. And you should also ask acquaintances who are attorneys and CPAs whom they have worked with on client matters. Whom have they have found to be particularly strategic and of high integrity? You should also do a bit of Internet research so that you have names to test. It's quite instructive to search terms like *wealth manager* or *financial advisor* for your area and see which names pop up. That way, as you ask others for recommendations, you have an opportunity to test names as well. For example, you would say to your tax accountant, "Have you ever heard of or worked with so and so?" Sometimes you can learn a lot hearing whom they don't work with and why. In other times it can help jog memories as to who might be worthy of your consideration.

In some communities you'll find that the choice is overwhelmingly one or two firms. In other areas you'll find that there are many reputable wealth management firms. Some suggest that you try to talk to at least three, but that really depends on how you like to approach things. It can be perfectly acceptable just to talk to one firm as long as you have been able to independently verify from enough people that they are truly a top choice.

So whether you are talking to one firm or many, here is what you might want to know about the potential wealth advisor:

Approach

- What kind of clients do they serve? Are they business owners or executives or community leaders like you? What is their experience with retirement transitions? How wealthy are their clients?
- How do they like to begin an engagement? What can you expect in the first year? They should be able to give you a timeline of the important milestones you can expect as you work together.
- What kind of client problems do they most like to solve? Granted, with client confidentiality you should not expect to hear specific war stories about individual clients (and if you do, be concerned about that). However, most can describe the kinds of client projects and challenges they most like to address. Be concerned if all they want to talk about is picking a great stock.
- Do they serve other clients like you? In particular you want to avoid being someone's largest client or smallest client. They might do a great job—but because of learning curve issues, they also might not. Go with someone whose clients are very similar to you. You want to be in their sweet spot.

Skill and Expertise

• What kind of training and credentialing do they have? Look for Certified Public Accountants, Certified Financial Planners, Chartered Financial Analysts, and others whose credentials require rigorous training.
• What do they do to stay current? The financial landscape changes quickly. Expect to hear that they go to industry conferences and attend continuing education programs. Most professions require a minimum number of hours each year. Bonus points are awarded if they also lecture, write, or teach.
• How long have they been at this? And with whom? You don't necessarily need an advisor with gray hair (in fact, having someone younger means they are more likely to still be working as you age), but it is good if they are associated with people who do have gray hair—as colleagues or partners. Best yet is someone who is affiliated with a firm of long standing. Good people do change firms from time to time, but you want to know how often they have changed firms. It's not a good sign if someone has moved frequently.

Substance

• What is the business model? You want to understand how they make money and who regulates them. For example, most wealth advisors operate as Registered Investment Advisors (RIAs), which means they collect fees based on either assets or service and that they are regulated by the Securities and Exchange Commission (SEC). More and more leading wealth advisors are also affiliated with trust companies, so that they can provide their clients with services today and for future generations. A trust company is a type of bank and will be supervised by either state or federal regulators. You will also find individuals practicing as wealth advisors within brokerage houses and traditional banks.
• Where will your funds be held? Will there be a separate custodian and some form of asset verification? The goal is for the advisors to still be able to do their job but to keep your assets safeguarded. We believe you want an outside custodian or a trust company as extra layers of protection. If the advisor or their firm will hold your funds directly, what are the checks and balances to make sure that there are no abuses of privilege?
• What kind of errors and omissions insurance do they carry? These policies don't need to be huge, but it is important that the organization have such coverage. If they appear offended by this question, you should be concerned.
• Do they appear to be profitable? This may seem like an odd question, but it is actually very important. You are always best served by working with a

profitable and substantial business that will be around for the long haul. It isn't just about safety. Wealth advisors need to be able to reinvest in technology, research, and other tools to continuously improve how they serve their clients. They are unlikely to do this if their business is not successful.

Compliance

• And what about regulatory matters? In the investment advisory world there is a required function called *compliance*. Whether the regulators are the SEC or state banking authorities or FINRA, all require the organization to maintain policies and procedures to ensure compliance with regulations and protect the consumer. We suggest you ask about the compliance function. Who is the chief compliance officer?
• Has the individual or their firm ever been sanctioned in any manner by regulators? Of course, in the case of any bad actor you can't be sure that this is been answered honestly, so you may want to check independently.

Compensation and Conflicts

• How does the advisor get paid? Clearly you want an advisor whose interests are as closely aligned with your own as possible. We suggest you search for a fee-only advisor, rather than someone who receives commissions as compensation.
• Who else might benefit from the advisor's recommendations? Some advisors have business relationships or partnerships that can affect the independence and objectivity of the advice they give you. For example, some firms have cost-sharing arrangements with vendors called *soft dollars*. These are not necessarily a bad thing, but you do want to be aware of them. The SEC requires them to be listed on Form ADV.
• Are they tied to specific products? Some firms also have proprietary products, like money market funds, where you are charged additional fees on top of what you pay your advisor. It's not the additional fee we worry about here (there are costs to all these things), it is whether or not the advisor is offering you the best possible choice. Are they required or inclined to use their firm's own product? Do they get a bigger bonus or a free trip if they place your assets in affiliated funds? No compensation structure is perfect, but a situation where the advisor is compensated only by you as a client is as good as it gets.

Chemistry

• Do you like the person? This is pretty fundamental. In the best scenario you'll be dealing with this person for many years. Will they wear well?

- Do they follow the team approach? If so, can you meet the other proposed members of the team? You should also clarify the roles of each team member. You want to be certain that the wealth advisor and analysts you meet with are those you will be dealing with.
- Is there any trace of condescension? It's our experience that condescension often covers a lack of expertise. Some would rather act as though your question is foolish rather than admit they cannot answer it. It can also be a cover for venality (think Bernie Madoff). Or it can be evidence of sexism or bigotry. Sometimes this can be subtle. In meetings with your spouse, are comments addressed to both of you? And are both of your questions given equal weight? We believe it is perfectly okay for someone to say to you, "You know, I don't have the answer to that question, but I will find it for you." But it is never okay for someone to belittle your question or urge you to do things that you don't understand and that they cannot properly explain.

Outcomes and Results

- Can this advisor deliver the things you need? They should be able to show you examples of their work product, both financial planning reports and performance analysis. You should expect to see a strong ability to do the kind of long-range personal financial forecasting we talk about in sustainability analysis. You should also expect to see examples of detailed performance reporting that allow you to remain very informed about what's working and what's not in your investment portfolio.
- Can they clearly articulate their investment approach? And are you comfortable with it? You want to look for an advisor who's got a comprehensive, detailed, and disciplined approach, someone who can talk about the overall portfolio rather than just the current hot investment vehicle.
- Do they select investment managers and mutual funds or do they select individual securities? In today's world it is difficult to get adequate diversification with the portfolio made up solely of individual stocks and bonds selected by one person. Rather, you should be searching for someone who will bring in a variety of investment approaches to you, based on research and due diligence.
- What kind of research capability do they have? Does the advisor do research on their own? Or do they have access to skilled researchers in-house? And what kind of research is done? The research should encompass forward-looking economic projections, reviews of global asset classes, potential impacts of tax law changes on investing, as well as detailed review of current and potential recommended investment

managers or mutual funds. This goes significantly beyond the typical research, which is based on individual stocks.

- What can they tell you about their investment performance? In the wealth management world it can be difficult to get detailed investment performance because of regulatory issues. What you want to know most of all is how the advisor has performed for other clients like you. A composite return that shows the results for every client they have may not be that revealing as it includes both their conservative clients and aggressive clients. Look for some breakout by client objective.

Meet Face-to-Face

With these questions at hand we strongly recommend that you meet face-to-face with the potential advisor multiple times. You may have an initial meeting that is nothing short of love at first sight. But this is such a big decision that it is clearly worth the time to meet two to three times to be sure you have the right fit.

Get It in Writing

It should not surprise you that our final recommendation is to get it in writing. You should be presented with a written contract and also any required regulatory disclosures in advance of the point where you're expected to sign them. We suggest that you ask the advisor to walk you through the contract and point out to you what they think are its essential elements. Specifically ask what happens should you decide to part company with the advisor. Then go away and read it before you do sign.

So clearly this is a big decision, selecting a wealth manager. We hope you find our comments helpful as you make this important choice. And may this relationship serve you well for many years to come.

Below is a list of all these questions in a more concise format to make it easier for you to conduct your interview.

Approach

- What kind of clients do they serve?
- How do they like to begin an engagement?
- What kind of client problems do they most like to solve?

Skill and Expertise

- What kind of training and credentialing do they have?
- How long have they been at this? And with whom?

Substance

- What is the business model?
- Where will your funds be held?
- What kind of errors and omissions insurance do they carry?
- Do they appear to be profitable?

Compliance

- Who is the chief compliance officer?
- Has the individual or their firm ever been sanctioned in any manner by regulators?

Compensation and Conflicts

- How does the advisor get paid?
- Who else might benefit from the advisor's recommendations?
- Are they tied to specific products?

Chemistry

- Do you like the person?
- Do they follow the team approach?
- Is there any trace of condescension?

Outcomes and Results

- Can this advisor deliver the things you need?
- Can the advisor clearly articulate their investment approach? And are you comfortable with it?
- Do they select investment managers or do they select individual securities?
- What kind of research capability do they have?
- What can they tell you about their investment performance?

Appendix 2: How to Vet a Personal Financial Forecast

Every good strategic plan has a forecast of the future. Your plan for your life needs one too. This type of forecast is often called a *sustainability analysis*, although there are other terms. Sustainability analysis is what we will call it here.

As with any business financial forecast, this look into the future is certain to be wrong in some aspect. It is the nature of the beast. What you are seeking from your analysis is to construct it in a way that is likely to be pretty much, mostly, or enough right to give you guidance for better decision making. You will find you refer to it frequently as you plot your future.

The core function of the sustainability analysis is actually fairly straightforward. It looks at available assets and expected cash receipts and matches them against desired expenditures to determine if your financial situation is sustainable over your lifetime. This would be easy if not for variables like inflation, risk, economic conditions, rates of return, and the like. In reality even your life expectancy is a variable if you think about it.

To get a useful sustainability analysis for purposes of planning requires three things:

- Good data to begin with.
- Thoughtful and realistic assumptions about variability.
- A robust mathematical engine to mash it all up.

Start with Good Data

The data in the original input almost always begin with things that come from your personal books and records. Your analysis will only be as good as

145

the accuracy of your lists of assets and liabilities, and the realism of your expectations about what it actually costs you to live. This is a prime example of the classic "garbage in, garbage out" rule. It is worth your time to make sure that you provide your advisor with the best data possible.

In addition, you'll be asked to outline your goals and objectives. These goals and objectives become some of the many moving parts in the analysis. Again, they should be carefully considered: Are they really what you want to do? The more goals and objectives you insert into the plan, the more you increase the level of variability, which in turn can make the plan less reliable. This is a case where less may be more.

Do consider laying out your anticipated expenditures in some detail. Often those facing retirement are encouraged to look at retirement spending as if it is monolithic, meaning that you pick one amount and that's what you assume you spend for the remainder of your life. This is not how it really works. Research clearly indicates that in fact people tend to spend more early in retirement and less later in retirement. To be most thoughtful about this, break spending up into a couple of basic categories, providing your baseline cost of living and then layering on top of that any special and shorter-term expenditures. One example we frequently see is clients telling us that they plan to travel extensively from, say, age 60 to age 70, but then after that they expect a slowdown. This kind of layering makes your numbers more realistic.

And once you've given this data to your financial advisor, don't forget to give them updates if things have changed. There may be changes in your personal financial situation that they would have no way of knowing but that could affect the outcome of this analysis. To do your part, make sure that the data are always fresh.

Thoughtful and Realistic Assumptions

They're called assumptions because you don't actually know what's going to happen. Assumptions by their nature are hypothetical. What you want is to be sure that the most educated "best guess" has been made in all key areas of variability flowing into your analysis. One may have a tendency to want to err on the side of conservatism or optimism. Either tendency yields a flawed result, so with every assumption you want to ask yourself if you think it is reasonable.

The key areas where assumptions will be used are:

Inflation—Be sure there is an assumption about inflation that makes sense to you. Do be aware that most people overestimate what future inflation is likely to look like. Times of hyperinflation are rare and usually short-lived. In most cases an inflation rate of around 2 percent is used.

Rates of return—This will be one of the most complex areas where assumptions are made. Now that we have the computer capability to run more complex models into the future, most analytical software is very robust when it comes to calculating returns. Generally you will see a breakout of the investments by asset class, assigning projected returns and projected risk to each specific asset class. These data can then be manipulated to provide returns based on historical returns or the advisor's economic perspective. Ask to be certain that some form of expense adjustments have been applied to rates of return to provide a realistic estimate of actual investment costs. Sometimes advisors use straight index data, but in reality there are always some expenses in actual investing.

Anticipating risk—As mentioned before, assumptions regarding risk are attached to each of the specific asset classes. As the models are run, some method is used to test what happens if returns do not turn out as expected. The risk assumptions provide parameters for those swings. In simple terms one asset class could provide expected returns of 3 percent but be assigned risk assumptions that they're not likely to be less than 1 percent or more than 5 percent at any time. Another asset class might have an expected return of 10 percent, but could also return over 25 percent or −5 percent, leaving a wider range of variability.

Life expectancy—This is the one area where we do suggest that you be a little bit conservative. If a life expectancy table suggests you are going to live to 83, you might want to tack a few years onto that. Or perhaps your own genetics have given you an indication. If both your parents are already in their late 90s, maybe you want to stretch it out a bit farther.

A Robust Financial Engine

The state of the art for preparing sustainability analyses is a thing called *Monte Carlo simulation*. A Monte Carlo simulation calculates the results of your plan by running it multiple times, each time using a different sequencing of returns. The goal is to simulate as many different possible economic scenarios as possible. It shouldn't be surprising that in some of the sequences your plan works beautifully and your financial situation is sustainable, and in other sequences it's not. With a Monte Carlo simulation, your desire is to run enough sequences to determine how likely overall your plan is to be successful.

In the simplest terms, say the simulation calculates the results of your returns 10,000 times, and 8,000 of those are successful. Then in Monte Carlo terms you are 80 percent confident that your plan will work. This is called either a *confidence level* or a *probability of success*. The goal as we define it is to achieve a confidence level of at least 75 percent. Interestingly, you actually may not want a confidence level that's too high; it may mean that you're not spending enough money or that you should consider making gifts during your lifetime.

What we have given you here is a fairly elementary explanation of what really goes on under the hood. Some of the mathematical engines used work in a variety of different ways. But all have the same goal: helping you determine how confident you can be about your financial future. We urge you to spend time with your advisor to gain at least a rudimentary understanding of how the engine works.

And finally, remember that all financial forecasts are blunt instruments. Do not expect pinpoint precision, and don't expect to rerun the analysis every time there's a relatively small change in your financial situation. We recommend rerunning it every 12 to 18 months or when something significant happens in your personal life that calls for a change in assumptions. Do use this analysis in a way that gives you peace of mind over the long run. That's why they call it a confidence level.

Appendix 3: Cash Flow Management

Once you retire, managing your personal cash flow changes significantly. Before retirement, the structures of regular salary and bonus payments often provided a natural metering function. In most cases, during your earning years you would be adding to savings and investments. And you simply have less time to spend money, anyway. All that changes when you quit working.

Now you'll want to be sure you are stewarding your cash more intentionally. Once you begin to spend out of investment income, you want to be sure that you have the control that you need not to draw down too quickly. We believe the first line of financial defense during retirement is carefully managing the cash that comes your way. The choices you make about that cash, where you consume it or invest it, can make or break even the best plan.

Part of why controlling cash is so difficult is that it is so liquid. Remember, liquid assets are those that can be spent easily, and cash is the most liquid asset there is. We have found that the secret to successful cash management is to make it as difficult as possible to spend money. The longer you can keep your dollars working for you, the better off you are. This will be the foundation of what we suggest for your cash management program.

Perhaps you already have a disciplined approach to spending money. Some people are most comfortable when they keep detailed records of all their expenditures. Others have a more relaxed approach, yet still watch their spending. It is unlikely that you will make a substantial change in your recordkeeping habits in retirement. If you already keep track, you will continue to keep track. If you don't, you're not likely to start now. What's important is to make sure you have some way of knowing when you are spending too much so that you can correct the problem immediately.

We definitely believe that it is unreasonable to expect yourself to begin a strict family budget at this point in your life if you were not in the habit of doing so. Yet you do need some sense of what it costs to live as a way of estimating needs into the future. You already did this work if you calculated your lifestyle costs as described in Chapter 7. The system you will use to manage cash is really very simple. We like to think it's elegantly simple. It is designed to mimic getting a paycheck every month, which for most people makes planning for personal spending much easier.

Here's how it works. Working with your advisor, set up a central collection account for all incoming cash. This is not your checking account or any account that you spend out of; it should be completely separate. Usually this is some type of a market rate bank or money fund account where your cash can earn some interest. Everything goes in it. This includes pension checks, Social Security, distributions from an IRA, consulting fees, or whatever else you have coming in. This is also where your advisor will help you keep your designated emergency fund.

From this collection account you will then set up automated transfers each month to your checking or spending account. Ideally you will figure out the different amount needed for each month well in advance. For example, you may need more in the months that you pay property taxes or school tuitions and less in other months. The amount to be transferred should be only the amount you plan to spend in any particular month. If organizing all this sounds daunting, be sure you turn to your advisor for help. Most organize this type of structured cash flow for their clients on a regular basis and can make this easy for you.

Once the planned amount has been transferred to your checking account to pay monthly living expenses, you should treat it like a finite paycheck. It is what you have to spend and you don't go beyond it except in extraordinary circumstances, managing your personal expenses in the same way you always have. It's that easy and that straightforward.

Depending upon what stage of retirement you're in and how much income you have coming in, you may also need to tap into your investments. This is also best done in a planned and strategic way. By looking at this prospectively with your advisor a plan can be devised to keep your investments working as long as possible but still regularly and adequately funding your cost of living. Any proceeds coming out of your investment accounts should also flow directly through the central collection account.

The accompanying diagram shows how all this works.

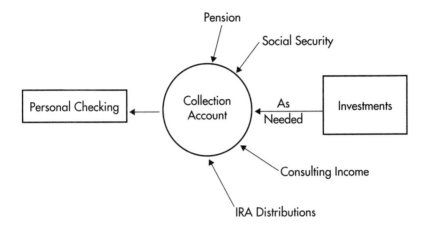

The diagram shows the most common form of this scheme. Of course, there are variations. As an example, perhaps as part of a couple you each like to have your own spending accounts. This is easily accommodated by having the automated transfers split in some form between the two accounts. Or perhaps your tax advisor has recommended that you set up a separate account for rental or consulting income. In those cases, then, the net proceeds are transferred to the central collection account. It still works just fine.

The bottom line is to create an environment that leaves you feeling in control of your finances. This is one way we have found that works for many clients. We hope you'll find it useful as well.

Appendix 4: Wealth Regeneration Interview Format

Name:

Date of interview:

How interviewee was identified:

1. Describe your career:
   a. Title:
   b. Career trajectory:

   c. What you loved about it:

   d. Philosophy of leading people:

2. What/when was your transition?

How did it go?_____

_____

_____

_____

_____

_____

3. How did you figure out what to do?_____

_____

_____

4. What else might have worked? (Road trip? Bolt from blue? Trial and error?
   Lost in the wilderness? Gap year? Or got lucky [there is no such thing]? Was
   there a crucible? Tragedy? Moral dilemma? Family situation?)

_____

_____

_____

_____

5. Did you have any kind of formal planning process?_____

_____

_____

6. Once you got fully engaged in your transition, how did it go?_____

_____

_____

7. What would you do differently?_____

_____

_____

_____

8. What advice do you have for others?_____

_____

_____

_____

Recommended Reading

If you would like to delve deeper into these subjects, here are some suggestions:

Bateson, Mary Catherine, *Composing a Further Life: The Age of Active Wisdom* (New York: Knopf, 2010).

Collier, Charles W., *Wealth in Families* (Cambridge: Harvard University Press, 2008).

Csikszentmihalyi, Mihaly, *Flow: The Psychology of Optimal Experience* (New York: HarperCollins, 2008).

Gary, Tracy with Nancy Adess, *Inspired Philanthropy: Your Step-by-Step Guide to Creating a Giving Plan and Leaving a Legacy* (San Francisco: Jossey-Bass, 2008).

George, Bill with Peter Sims, *True North: Discover Your Authentic Leadership* (San Francisco: Jossey-Bass, 2007).

George, Bill, Andrew McLean, and Nick Craig, *Finding Your True North: A Personal Guide* (San Francisco: Jossey-Bass, 2008).

Gersick, Kelin E., John A. Davis, Marion McCollom, and Ivan Lansberg, *Generation to Generation: Life Cycles of the Family Business* (Boston: Harvard Business School Press, 1997).

Hausner, Lee, and Douglas K. Freeman, *The Legacy Family: The Definitive Guide to Creating a Successful Multigenerational Family* (New York: Palgrave Macmillan, 2009).

Hughes, James E. Jr., *Family Wealth: Keeping It in the Family* (Princeton: Bloomberg Press, 2004).

Jaffe, Dennis T., *Stewardship in Your Family Enterprise: Developing Responsible Family Leadership Across Generations* (Pioneer Imprints, 2010).

Kotter, John P., and Dan S. Cohen, *The Heart of Change: Real-Life Stories of How People Change Their Organizations* (Boston: Harvard Business School Press, 2002).

Lawrence-Lightfoot, Sara, *The Third Chapter: Passion, Risk and Adventure in the 25 Years After 50* (New York: Sarah Crichton Books, 2009).

McLean, Pamela D., and Frederic M. Hudson, *LifeLaunch: A Passionate Guide to the Rest of Your Life* (Santa Barbara: Hudson Institute Press, 1995).

Sonnenfeld, Jeffrey, *The Hero's Farewell: What Happens When CEOs Retire* (New York: Oxford University Press, 1988).

Spence, Linda, Legacy: *A Step-by-Step Guide to Writing Personal History* (Athens: Swallow Press/Ohio University Press, 1997).

Stone, Douglas, Bruce Patton, and Sheila Heen, *Difficult Conversations: How to Discuss What Matters Most* (New York: Penguin Books, 1999).

Vaillant, George E., *Aging Well* (New York: Little, Brown & Company, 2002).

Weil, Andrew, *Healthy Aging: A Lifelong Guide to Your Well-Being* (New York: Anchor Books, 2005).

About the Authors

Kaycee Krysty

Kaycee Krysty's resume in financial planning spans more than 30 years. After seven years as CEO of Laird Norton Tyee, a Seattle-based wealth management firm, Kaycee transitioned to the newly created position of president emerita in early 2011. In this role, Kaycee is charged with researching and innovating strategies for individuals and families facing life transitions.

Kaycee's passion for helping individuals and families sprang from her own life experience. She learned firsthand as a teenager at the time of her father's accidental death that families need to be prepared for any eventuality.

Kaycee began her career as a CPA in 1977, ultimately becoming a partner with Moss Adams, one of the largest CPA firms in the United States. Throughout her career in public accounting, she stayed focused on the needs of individuals and private businesses.

In 1995, Kaycee saw a growing need of her clients for a better way to plan and invest their finances. They needed a partner with no conflicts of interest who could help them create financial strategies that helped them achieve their personal goals. She left Moss Adams to cofound Tyee Asset Strategies LLC, one of the first fee-only planning firms in the Pacific Northwest. Tyee grew rapidly, exceeding $1 billion in assets under management by early 2000.

In 2001, the majority interest in Tyee was purchased by Laird Norton Financial Group. The Laird Norton Family, now in their seventh generation as business owners, focuses heavily on the sustainability of their businesses and their family. They saw the planning strength and fee-only structure of Tyee as a great complement to the trust services they already provided family members and other prominent northwest clients. In turn, Kaycee saw this collaboration as an opportunity to make Tyee's service model sustainable for future generations. In 2004 a merger created Laird Norton Tyee. Today Laird Norton Tyee has over $4 billion in assets under advisement.

Throughout her career, Kaycee threw herself wholeheartedly into her work. She was recognized six times by *Worth* magazine on its list of "Best Financial Advisors in the United States." She is the former chair of the American Institute of CPAs Personal Financial Planning Division. Locally she was honored in 2006 as one of *Puget Sound Business Journal*'s Women of Influence and has been named a Five-Star Wealth Manager™ multiple times.

Rising to the role of CEO of the company she helped create was a dream come true for Kaycee. She loved her work, her clients, and her colleagues. Transition was the furthest thing from her mind—that is, until she got a big bump of reality.

In 2007 she was diagnosed with breast cancer and not just one tumor but two. Only two years before, she had been at USC Medical Center in Los Angeles to get a benign but dangerous tumor removed from the base of her brain. Now there's a wake-up call (or two), or at least it should have been. Yet it was not until the experience of the cancer treatment—particularly the chemotherapy in 2008—that her health finally got her attention. It was her crucible moment. Suddenly, thoughts about her own legacy burst into high relief. If not now, when? And what? The wheel began to turn.

Now cancer free, Kaycee quickly recognized that this was the right time in her life to go back to doing what she loved the most: spending hands-on time researching and creating leading-edge financial planning solutions, the kinds of solutions that help people embrace whatever is next in life. She knew she wanted to teach and write as well. This pushed her to recognize that the 24/7 nature of the CEO's role was no longer a good fit. And that it was time to get serious about a succession plan.

After a nationwide search, Bob Moser was brought in as chief client service officer and president of Laird Norton Tyee in the fall of 2008. Kaycee and Bob worked side by side for over two years, through difficult economic times, to prepare the way for his leadership and her new path. That period of careful planning, thought, and collegiality yielded a smooth transition for the company that Kaycee loves so much. And this in turn left her free to follow her purpose.

Today Kaycee remains working side by side with Bob on many of the things that are important to Laird Norton Tyee's clients as they seek successful and sustainable futures. The difference now is that she gets to sleep in; spend more time with her husband, Michael; her dogs get longer walks; and she can gracefully exit the room when operational matters surface. She has the freedom and the time to dig deeply into the larger issues we all face as we age—legacy, purpose, meaning, and sustainability. *Wealth Regeneration at Retirement* is just one result; we expect to see many more.

Robert Moser

Bob Moser has more than 25 years of private wealth management, financial services, and business management experience. He is president and chief executive officer of Laird Norton Tyee, a Seattle-based registered investment advisor and trust company. Bob came to Laird Norton Tyee in 2008 as chief client service officer and president after a long career in banking where he rose to the senior executive ranks with SunTrust Banks, Inc. For the past 15 years, he has also advised a variety of private foundations in the areas of governance and strategic planning.

Bob is a member of several industry and not-for-profit organizations including the Trust Management Association and the Community Development Roundtable in Seattle. He serves on the board of directors for Amara, an adoption services agency in Seattle; College Success Foundation, which provides scholarships and mentoring for low-income, high-potential students; and he is the former chairman of the Children's Home Society of Florida.

Bob's own story is all about transitions, both planned and unplanned. When Bob was young, his father worked for DuPont. Every time his dad got a promotion, it meant moving to a new place to live (and his dad was very good at getting promotions). As a result, Bob lived in six different cities and attended as many different schools before he was in high school.

After completing school, Bob picked the financial services industry as a career because the common belief at the time was that it was a stable environment and he would probably work for the same company, in the same city, for his entire career.

Boy . . . was he completely wrong! Even though he stayed with the same company for most of his career, Bob was destined to follow in his father's footsteps. Bob and his family moved seven different times, the last six with the same company. Like his father, he was pretty good at getting promotions, but they always seemed to come with a move to a new city. Over the course of his career, the moves allowed Bob to manage a wide range of wealth management and investment banking businesses. He served as chief risk officer and chief strategy officer for SunTrust's Wealth & Investment Management line of business, and he was president of SunTrust's Delaware Trust Company. In addition, Bob also served as president of Asset Management Advisors in Orlando, Florida, a SunTrust affiliate.

Bob eventually landed in Atlanta as a senior corporate executive taking a series of jobs that can best be described as "corporate fireman," and he loved it. Unfortunately, they also took him farther away from what he really loved about the business: making an impact in the lives of his clients. Bob couldn't see it but his wife, Candy, sure did. When the opportunity to join Laird Norton Tyee came up, it was Candy's encouragement and gentle shove that forced Bob to consider what really was important. At Laird Norton Tyee, Bob would have the opportunity to not only impact his clients' lives, but he would be helping shape the future of a vibrant family-owned business.

For Bob, this was exactly the "bump" of the wheel described in the book. Bob was comfortable and successful and his wheel was working perfectly well, thank you very much. It was the bump and the gentle push that sent the wheel forward to discover new opportunities and reconnect to what was important.

You spend just 10 minutes with Bob today, and you learn that the wheel has come to rest in a wonderful place. He wakes up excited, thinking about what's next for his clients and the business he loves. And he still has his eyes open for when the next bump will happen!

Index

161

About Laird Norton Tyee

Laird Norton Tyee is one of the Pacific Northwest's largest, privately held wealth management firms, with nearly $4 billion in assets under advisement. Founded in 1967 to serve the financial management needs of the Laird and Norton families, the firm now serves more than 400 high-net-worth individuals, families, and foundations. As both a registered investment advisor and a deeply experienced trust company, Laird Norton Tyee has helped clients achieve long-term financial results, reach their personal goals, and leave lasting legacies.

Stay in touch!